Gospel-Centred Youth Work and Ministry

John Caldwell

DEDICATION

To the 'non-professionals' who are faithful in caring
for young people, serving them well, and sharing
the faith.

Contents

ACKNOWLEDGMENTS

Thanks to my wife, Laura, for feedback at various stages of the manuscript. Thanks to Richard Coull for all the graphic work, and for having a Kingdom approach to business. Thanks to Allan Clyne, who, while not always (rarely) agreeing with me, has encouraged me along the way and provided constructive feedback at various points. Thinking beyond the manuscript itself, I would also like to thank John McMurray and Graham Curry for all their support and encouragement in the early years of my youth work experience.

COMMENDATIONS

"This is no reactionary summons to traditionalism but a well-reasoned analysis of the weakness of the contemporary scene and of the key elements to faithful, relevant youth work."
Ivor MacDonald: Minister, Hope Church Coatbridge

"This is a book that's clearly Gospel-focused and thoroughly biblical: John wants to keep the Bible and the Gospel firmly at the centre of youth work."
Phil Moon

"I have found 'Gospel-Centred Youth Work' very refreshing. The insights are encouraging. I found the quotes inspiring and overall it has helped me refocus which is a blessing from God."
Brian Lowrie: MAD Ministries

Introduction

Gospel-Centred Youth Work and Ministry is an exploration of two of the major contemporary approaches to working with young people. However before I begin to introduce the various methods of youth work and ministry, I need to mention something of the wider context which has led to the development of contemporary approaches to youth work and ministry. Phillip Ryken and James Montgomery Boice have argued that: 'The evangelical movement has lost its grip on the gospel.'[1] Boice and Ryken demonstrate that the evangelical movement has lost its distinctive identity because it has bowed down to the cultural pressures of the world. Boice and Ryken identify six major cultural trends which have influenced and shaped evangelicalism. These trends are secularism, humanism, relativism, materialism, pragmatism, and anti-intellectualism (or mindlessness). These terms are defined as follows:

> Secularism is the view that the universe is all there is; God and eternity are excluded. Humanism is the belief that – in the words of the ancient pagan philosophers – "Man is the measure of all things." This inevitably leads to worship of self. Relativism teaches that because there is no God, there are no absolutes; truth is relative. Materialism is closely related to secularism. If nothing exists except the here and now, then the meaning of life can be found only in possessions. Pragmatism measures truth by

---

[1] James Montgomery Boice, Phil Ryken, *The Doctrines of Grace: Rediscovering the Evangelical Gospel*, (Wheaton Illinois: Crossway, 2002), 20.

its practical utility. What is right and true is whatever works. Mindlessness is the overall "dumbing down" of popular culture, the shrinking of the American mind, which television has done a great deal to accelerate.[2]

Boice and Ryken's book demonstrates the numerous ways in which evangelicalism is characterised by these six cultural trends. It is important to understand this wider context because this is the context in which Christian youth work and ministry have emerged. In other words, Christian youth work and ministry have been birthed by a church movement which has been severed from its historical and biblical roots. Consequently, Christian youth work and ministry are being increasingly shaped by cultural influences which are undermining the very Christian faith that they are attempting to promote.

Discussions about professional values and Christianity often focus on evangelism versus social action; this, however, can be misleading. The conflict in Christian youth work and ministry is not about social action versus evangelism; it is about the gospel versus humanism. Consequently, a gospel-centred approach to Christian youth work will cut against the grain of contemporary principles and methods.

It is my prayer and hope that this book will raise a deeper awareness of the contemporary practices which undermine the gospel of the Lord Jesus Christ. At times the tone is sharp, and it needs to be. When the heartbeat of mission disappears from our Christian ministry, we do not need a tonic to soothe us, we need a defibrillator to revive us.

---

[2] Boice and Ryken, 21.

1 Mixed Messages

Two of the most common approaches to working with young people, certainly within evangelicalism, are *Christian youth work* and *youth ministry*. Christian youth work draws its principles and practice from secular youth work (informal education) and many of its projects are financed by secular funders. Christian youth work has developed its own profession, degree programmes and accreditation for youth workers.

On the other hand, Christian youth ministry is less specialised and is usually funded by the church. Youth work tends to focus on personal and social development, whereas youth ministry tends to focus on providing alternative activities for church youth in order to keep them in church and away from the world. Youth ministry will also have more of a focus on evangelism and discipleship. Both youth ministry and Christian youth work operate within local churches or para-church organisations.[3]

For approximately ten years, I was involved in both Christian youth work and youth ministry, I have worked with young people in the context of the local church and para-church. In all of these settings, I have worked with teams of staff and volunteers who are passionate about making a difference in the lives of young people. I have seen

---

[3] For a more detailed and expanded discussion of the varying purposes of Christian youth work and ministry, see Appendix: What's the Point?

the blessing of God in the various projects and I have experienced the joy of seeing young people develop and grow in each of these environments. However, in all of these contexts, I have also observed similar problems and weaknesses.

One major weakness is that professional Christian youth work and Christian youth ministry have a tendency to present mixed messages when it comes to communicating the Christian faith. In slightly different ways, both approaches to communicating the gospel are conditioned by the values of non-Christian culture. Very often, the messages presented to young people are a mixture of Christianity and humanism. Professional Christian youth work has shied away from a universally applicable and authoritatively true gospel whereas youth ministry is so desperate to be accepted by youth culture that it simply repackages the values and beliefs of non-Christian culture and tries to present them as Christianity.

In youth ministry, the clear gospel message tends to be obscured in a cloud of cultural confusion. While there is some attempt to explain the gospel to young people, it is hidden in a maze of cultural jargon, assumptions and competing priorities. For example, one youth ministry believes that:

> In every single person there is a sleeping giant called potential. This potential represents greatness and a CHAMPION spirit in everyone.

Consequently their ministry is aimed at 'releasing and inspiring a generation of Champions!'

Another youth ministry aims to raise up a generation of young people who are: 'bold, daring, dangerous, unrestrained by convention, free-spirited, original or fearless, especially in challenging assumptions or conventions.' These are tremendous assertions, but what do they mean, and what do they have to do with the gospel of Jesus Christ? The answer to both questions is absolutely nothing. These declarations do, however, have everything to do with consumerist marketing techniques. They are full of spin and all the right buzz words that are designed to appeal to a generation of young people who are looking for affirmation, purpose and freedom.

Notice that these youth ministries are not looking to develop the characteristics of true spirituality within young people. There is no talk of raising up humble; self-denying; holy and righteous, submissive authority-respecting; non-glamorous Christians. Why is that? Quite simply, true spirituality doesn't market well.

In some contexts, the gospel message is not clouded by confusion: it is just completely compromised. Professional Christian youth work, for example, often leads to the compromise of core gospel convictions. The underpinning philosophy of moral relativism at the heart of informal education conflicts with the authority of the gospel as revealed through the scriptures. Informal education's commitment to relativism and rejection of Christianity on the basis of its absolute, universal and authoritative truth claims are clearly highlighted in informal educator Carole Pughe's article: "Christian Youth work: Evangelism or Social action?"

> The postmodernist critique challenged the Christian conception of 'truth', by demanding the acceptance of plurality. For evangelicals 'truth is a very clear-cut issue: something is either true in a fairly literal or

historical way or it is not true at all' (Tomlinson 1995: 87). Thus evangelical youth work adopts a legislative approach, seizing opportunities to define reality. While youth and community work is urged to adopt an interpretivist stance that recognises the role of spirituality amongst many.[4]

Pughe's article is raising the important contrast between the relativist worldview and the Christian worldview.

However, the Christian faith cannot be communicated faithfully in an informal education context because it is an absolute truth claim and informal education is committed to relativism which rejects absolute truth claims. Consequently, Christian youth workers who operate within an informal education framework must compromise the gospel. This compromise of the gospel is clearly seen in Pete Ward's work: 'Youth Culture and the Gospel':

> Reading the average guide to evangelism there seems to be an assumption that the Gospel is one simple and basic message which we should try to get over to people.[5]

Ward is challenging the fact that the gospel is one universal (applicable to all people at all times) message. He later uses the word 'formula' to describe the idea of a universal message (a term which no evangelical theologian would ever use) in order to deny the universality of the gospel. This

---

[4] Carole Pughe, "Christian Youth work: Evangelism or Social action?" Infed http://www.infed.org.uk/christianeducation/christianyw.htm (accessed 20th Nov 2013).

[5] Pete Ward, *Youth Culture and the Gospel,* (London: Marshall: Pickering, 1992), 115.

denial that the gospel is a universal message is at the heart of many professional Christian youth work approaches to 'spiritual development'. The reason for this is simple: it is the only way that a Christian professional youth worker can engage in conversations about the gospel without compromising the informal education commitment to relativism. However, in adopting this approach, Christian youth workers compromise the gospel in the process.

In order to justify his claims scripturally, Ward goes on to claim that:

'He [Jesus] did not preach according to the gospel formula I had been taught was universal and unchanging.'[6]

Ward is denying that there is such a thing as a universally applicable gospel. Ward tries to support this view by saying, 'Jesus says different things to different people.'[7] This of course is a careless and misleading approach to interpreting and applying the scriptures. The consistency between the message of the Old Testament prophets (including John the Baptist), Jesus, and the apostles, in preaching a universal and authoritative message is overwhelming. The scriptures, from Genesis to Revelation, are united in their testimony; the scriptures consistently demonstrate God's plan of salvation through Jesus Christ.

The message of Jesus (and the Old Testament Prophets)

Then he said to them, "These are my words that I spoke to you while I was still with you, that

---

[6] Ward, 116.
[7] Ward, 116.

everything written about me in the Law of Moses
and the Prophets and the Psalms must be fulfilled."
Then he opened their minds to understand the
Scriptures, and said to them, "Thus it is written,
that the Christ should suffer and on the third day
rise from the dead, and that repentance and
forgiveness of sins should be proclaimed in his
name to all nations, beginning from Jerusalem.
(Luke 24:44-47)

The message of the apostles

For I delivered to you as of first importance what I
also received: that Christ died for our sins in
accordance with the Scriptures, that he was buried,
that he was raised on the third day in accordance
with the Scriptures. (1 Cor 15: 3-4)

What has been the focus of God's messengers
throughout salvation history? It is the message of
salvation through God's redeemer who is fully
revealed in the New Testament as the Lord Jesus
Christ. Jesus Christ is the great theme of the Old
Testament, the Prophets, Christ himself and the
Apostles.

Consider John the Baptist's message: 'Behold,
the Lamb of God, who takes away the sin of the
world!' (John 1: 29) Consider the words of Christ
regarding the great theme of the scriptures: 'You
search the Scriptures because you think that in
them you have eternal life; and it is they that bear
witness about me.' (John 5:39) The message of the
apostles is equally consistent: 'But we preach Christ
crucified.' (1 Cor 1:23) Ward is clearly mistaken
when he denies a universal gospel, and Christian
Youth work clearly misses the mark when it fails to
present a universal gospel to young people.

Why do Christian youth workers, like Ward, work so hard to claim that there is no universal gospel? It would seem they do so in order to avoid the fact that they do not preach the universal gospel. They do not preach what Jesus preached. They do not preach the apostolic gospel; to do so would be to compromise their commitment professional and secular values.

During my time in theological college, (while training in Christian youth work), the youth workers were in the games room while the theology students were worshipping in the chapel. One of the youth workers was having a meltdown: 'How is *that* relevant to young people?' he exclaimed, pointing towards the chapel where worshippers were singing 'Amazing Grace'.

This youth worker was not being controversial, he was clearly troubled and finding it difficult to reconcile the professional values with the historic Christian faith. Tragically, in the process, he was losing sight of what it was all about. His work with young people (which was successful), along with his studies, which focused on relevance and relativism, was causing him to lose sight of the relevance of God's grace. This is one of the greatest challenges for Christian youth work and ministry. The present need is not to discover new ways to make the gospel relevant, but to rediscover that the gospel *is* relevant.

Most of the youth ministry gospel messages I have heard from countless platforms for over a decade seem to focus on the same issues. Surprisingly, for all the noise about diversity and creativity, youth ministry messages tend to be narrowly focused on the following areas.

Self-esteem

The self-esteem gospel finds its scriptural justification in the first two chapters of Genesis which speak of humans being made in God's image. This message recognises that many adolescents struggle with self-esteem issues and offers the gospel as a way in which young people can feel better about themselves. This version of the gospel speaks about how valuable young people are to God and encourages them to see themselves as special to God.

What is the problem with this? I am not denying the value of humanity to God; however, I am arguing that this message, in and of itself, is not the gospel, neither was it the teaching of Jesus or the apostles. This approach seems to ignore the fact that while God made humans in his own image, there was in fact a fall. Consequently, humans are in rebellion against God and actively reject his purposes. Humanity has fallen very far short of the glory we were intended to reflect.

As a result of this approach, young people are led to believe that the root of their problems is their emotions, but the problem is much deeper. Sin affects the whole being: body, mind, will, emotions and spirit. Not only does this approach fail to identify young people's true problem, it provides the wrong solution. The answer is not found in believing we are special to God, the answer is found in the cross of Christ. The 'I'm special' message may pull on the emotional strings of young people but it actually undermines the true love of God which is manifest through the cross. However, before a person can understand their need of the cross, they must understand their sin in the light of God's holiness. John Stott demonstrates this principle effectively: "Before we can begin to see the cross as something done for us we have to see it as something done by us."[8]

Purpose

The universal gospel of youth ministry is the message of purpose and fulfilment: 'God has a wonderful plan for your life.' is possibly the most popular gospel message pouring forth from youth ministry platforms. Again this is not the whole story, but it is used by many youth ministries to motivate and inspire young people, John Stott again challenges this type of message:

> Either we preach that human beings are rebels against God, under his just judgment and lost, and that Christ crucified who bore their sin and curse is the only available Saviour. Or we emphasize human potential and human ability, with Christ brought in only to boost them, and with no necessity for the cross except to exhibit God's love and so inspire us to great endeavour.[9]

Once again the 'God's plan for our life' message misses the real issue of human sin and rebellion. It misses the fact that people are sinners in need of a saviour.

God's love

Ask many youth ministries what the message of the gospel is and they will say something about 'helping people to experience God's love.' In youth ministry, as with wider evangelicalism, the word

---

[8] John Stott, *The Cross of Christ* (Downers Grove, IL, IVP, 1986), (Kindle Edition).
[9] Stott, (Kindle).

'love' has become devoid of any meaning. This approach misrepresents God: it ignores the fact that God is not only love; He is also holy and all powerful. Consequently, there is very little fear of God to be found in youth ministry contexts, but there is instead a nauseating emphasis on me-centred messages.

In order to ensure that our message is God's message, we need to hold firmly to the gospel. We need be able to say with Paul: 'For I am not ashamed of the gospel, for it is the power of God for salvation to everyone who believes.' (Rom 1:16) Before we can share this message with young people, the power of the message must have touched our own lives.

As missionaries we are messengers and our message is not 'This is what I think...' but, 'Here is what God says...' The apostles understood the importance of demonstrating not just the truthfulness of their message but also the divine source (and therefore the authoritative nature) of their message.

> For I would have you know, brothers, that the gospel that was preached by me is not man's gospel. For I did not receive it from any man, nor was I taught it, but I received it through a revelation of Jesus Christ. (Gal 1:11-12)

In this passage Paul is writing to a church which has abandoned the apostolic gospel and has embraced a false gospel. In order to bring the church back on course, Paul appeals to the fact that there is only one true gospel and emphasises that it is not a human invention or personal perspective. Having established the authoritative nature of the true gospel, Paul goes on to warn about the consequence of compromising the true gospel:

> I am astonished that you are so quickly deserting him who called you in the grace of Christ and are turning to a different gospel— not that there is another one, but there are some who trouble you and want to distort the gospel of Christ. But even if we or an angel from heaven should preach to you a gospel contrary to the one we preached to you, let him be accursed. As we have said before, so now I say again: If anyone is preaching to you a gospel contrary to the one you received, let him be accursed.(Gal 1:6-9)

The plain speech of Paul is too much for the postmodern palate. Such thinking is considered primitive, oppressive and narrow-minded. However, while Paul's way of speaking may not be popular, if we are engaged in Christian youth work or ministry, we need to take these warnings very seriously. If we speak about the things of God to young people, we need to be faithful to communicate what He has spoken. Youth workers and youth leaders are constantly living with the pressure of trying to be popular. The success of their work depends upon young people *choosing* to engage with their activities; therefore, youth workers and leaders try to offer something that is appealing to youth. The major problem for youth workers and ministers is that the gospel does not appeal to fallen human nature. The apostles understood this; they recognised that the gospel was an offense to many, 'For the word of the cross is folly to those who are perishing, but to us who are being saved it is the power of God.' (1 Cor 1:18) One of the faulty premises of Christian youth work and ministry is the idea that people reject Christianity because the church has failed to make

Jesus attractive. While this may be true in some cases (where churches are either legalistic or liberal), scripture actually gives us a clearer reason for why people reject the gospel: 'The god of this world has blinded the minds of the unbelievers, to keep them from seeing the light of the gospel of the glory of Christ, who is the image of God.' (2 Cor 4:4) Young people do not reject Christ because the church is not cool, young people reject Christ because by nature they are spiritually blind.

The misunderstanding of the human condition has led many youth ministries to devise endless methods and strategies to try to win the lost. They have thrown out the gospel as irrelevant and have tried to win a generation of young people with hype, entertainment and positive thinking. Christian youth ministries need to move from gimmick-centred ministry to gospel-centred ministry.

Like many things in life, the right solution can only be found if we understand the problem. Many youth ministries have spent countless hours looking for the cultural reasons as to why young people reject Christ. Countless assumptions have followed: 'Church is boring', 'The message is irrelevant', 'There's no music', 'The music isn't my style' and so on. Consequently superficial solutions have been manufactured: entertaining services, person-centred preaching, introduction of worship bands, followed by rock concert styled worship services, rave music worship services, and hip hop worship services. Yet these ministries have missed the real problem: blind men don't see and dead men don't worship. God hasn't called us to do what can be done by human engineering; he has called us to the impossible. He has called us to open the eyes of the blind and raise the dead.

One of the least popular ideas within Christian youth work is the idea that the gospel is a universal message. A great deal of emphasis is placed upon the sociological and cultural contexts that young people find themselves within; it is argued that there is no 'one size fits all' when it comes to the gospel. Of course, there is a degree of truth in this argument; the missionary must attempt to build relationships and understand something of the culture of the young people they are seeking to reach. A major part of the argument of this book draws attention to the prevalent worldviews within society and how they impact young people, youth work and ministry. However, in seeking to understand the culture, we are seeking ways in which we can communicate the gospel within the culture. In other words, there is one thing we are seeking to communicate to all people in all places:

> And he said to them, "Go into all the world and proclaim the gospel to the whole creation. Whoever believes and is baptized will be saved, but whoever does not believe will be condemned. (Mark 16:15-16)

The gospel is a universal message because the world has a universal problem and this problem has universal consequences. The problem is sin; the consequence is judgement and wrath (in this life and in the life to come). The answer to this problem for all people in all places is Jesus Christ.

The gospel has always and will always challenge every culture because every culture is dominated and tainted by sin. While contextualisation of the gospel to the point of redefining the gospel is justified on sociological grounds, it seems too obvious that many contextualised efforts have simply removed the offense of the gospel.

Removing the parts of the gospel which are unpopular (and which are assumed to lead people to reject the gospel) on the premise that they will now accept the gospel, is not effective mission, it is effective compromise.

Over-emphasis on contextualisation is a real problem for Christian youth work and ministry because it sends out a crystal clear message that the gospel is not sufficient or relevant. I have participated in countless youth work and ministry workshops and seminars which explored the issue of contextualisation and every time I was left with the impression that the person leading the session did not believe that the gospel is relevant. Over-emphasis on contextualisation is the major reason why youth workers and ministries have embraced unbiblical ideologies and methods in order to reach young people.

The main argument for contextualisation is based upon the idea that we must understand the world of the young person and meet them on their terms. I remember one youth worker, who was leading a national denominational seminar for youth leaders, claim that:

> Young people born approximately after 1999 are known to sociologists as the millennial generation. A characteristic of the millennial generation is that they don't want to be told what is true, they want to create truth.

Leaving aside the sociological assumptions for a moment, what was really concerning about this statement, was the fact that he made no attempt to demonstrate *how* the gospel challenges such a worldview. Instead, youth leaders representing their local churches on a nationwide scale were left with the impression that youth ministry is not about communicating truth to young people but is instead about enabling young people to create their own truth.

Resistance to objective truth and the desire to create one's own reality may well be a characteristic of the millennial generation, but to try to meet this worldview on its own terms is to abandon the very gospel we are seeking to communicate. This kind of thinking is similar to that of the Emergent Church which seeks to lay aside claims of absolute truth in order to reach a generation which rejects absolute truth. If we follow this approach, we no longer represent the truth but we ourselves have rejected the truth.

A further problem with basing youth ministry on sociological assumptions is that it creates superficial categories for young people. Rejection of truth and the perception of self as the source of truth may be characteristic of the millennial generation, but it is not unique to them, it has been characteristic of humanity since the fall:

> For the wrath of God is revealed from heaven against all ungodliness and unrighteousness of men, who by their unrighteousness suppress the truth. For what can be known about God is plain to them, because God has shown it to them. For his invisible attributes, namely, his eternal power and divine nature, have been clearly perceived, ever since the creation of the world, in the things that have been made. So they are without excuse. For although they knew God, they did not honour him as God or give thanks to him, but they became futile in their thinking, and their foolish hearts were darkened. (Rom 1:18-21)

If Christian youth work and ministry operated within a more gospel-centred approach, these fallacies regarding contextualisation could be avoided. Young people do not reject truth because they are teenagers, or because they were born in the millennium, like everyone else, they reject truth because they are sinners by nature: 'For the mind that is set on the flesh is hostile to God, for it does not submit to God's law; indeed, it cannot.' (Rom 8:7)

Identifying sin as the root cause of unbelief among young people is not popular in youth work and ministry contexts. I was once at a Christian youth event where some guys were leading rap workshops. The work shop itself was very good; the youth leaders connected well with the young people and the content of the raps was God-centred and biblical. In the closing session, one of the youth leaders invited the young people to attend one of the regular local youth clubs and proceeded to say, 'Don't worry, if you come along no one is going to preach to you or tell you that you're a sinner or anything like that, because that kind of thing is not good, is it?' Of course the non-Christian young people wholeheartedly agreed that hearing about 'sin' and 'preaching' was not a good thing.

In order to appeal to the young people, the youth worker wanted to distance himself from the negative stereotypes associated with church. Preaching and the doctrine of sin are abhorrent to a secular humanistic society. The very words are taboo in some circles. Yet despite the fact that preaching and the doctrine of sin are misrepresented and convey a negative image to many people, they are in fact an essential part of the Christian faith. It is only through preaching we will hear about Christ, and it is only through the doctrine of sin that we will understand our need of Christ.

Of course, youth clubs are not a church, and I am not arguing that they should be like a church. By their very nature, youth clubs and youth drop-in centres are more informal – and they need to be. I *am* arguing that youth work and youth ministry can adopt informal approaches without undermining the authority and teaching of the local church. I am also saying that youth workers are working against the gospel if they neglect, reject or attack the doctrine of sin.

So far in this chapter we have explored some of the key factors which cause the Christian message to become obscured within Christian youth work and ministry approaches. In doing so, we have touched on some of the core elements of the gospel which are downplayed, abandoned or undermined. Let us now turn to look at the essential elements of the gospel in more detail. If youth work and ministry send out mixed messages, the only way to correct this is to become clear about the essential marks of the gospel.

What is the gospel, anyway?

In a message entitled 'Sign of Times', A.W Pink declared that: "The nature of Christ's salvation is woefully misrepresented by the present-day "evangelist". He announces a Saviour from Hell, rather than a Saviour from sin." If this was true in the early 20th century, it is even more so today, because the 21st century evangelist preaches *neither* a saviour from hell *nor* a saviour from sin. The words of Robert Schuller encapsulate the modern day gospel perfectly: 'Jesus is my self-esteem booster.'

When youth ministry presents the gospel as a means of self-esteem, fulfilment and purpose, it seriously falls short of the apostolic gospel. J.I Packer demonstrates the danger of this approach to evangelism:

> We have all heard the Gospel presented as God's triumphant answer to human problems – problems of our relation with ourselves and our fellow humans and our environment. Well, there is no doubt that the Gospel does bring us solutions to these problems, but it does so by first solving a deeper problem – the deepest of all human problems, the problem of man's relation with His Maker. And unless we make it plain that the solution to the former problems depends on the settling of this latter, we are misrepresenting the message and becoming false witnesses of God – for a half-truth presented as if it were the whole truth becomes something of a falsehood by that very fact.[10]

Packer is arguing for the need for us to understand what the gospel actually accomplishes. He is highlighting the fact that we need to understand that the depth of the human problem is not loneliness, addiction, poor self-esteem or whatever else plagues us. As an evangelist once said, 'The heart of the human problem is the problem of the human heart.' The root problem for all of humanity is the fact that our sin has separated us from God. The great evangelist John Wesley gave young preachers this advice: 'Know your disease, know your cure.' J.I Packer helps us understand the depth of the human problem and God's plan of salvation in the following statement:

> By sin the New Testament means not social error or failure in the first instance, but rebellion against,

---

[10] J.I Packer, *Knowing God*, (Great Britain: Hodder and Stoughton, 1973), 213.

defiance of, retreat from and consequent guilt before God the Creator; and sin, says the New Testament, is the basic evil from which we need deliverance, and from which Christ died to save us. All that has gone wrong in human life between man and man is ultimately due to sin, and our present state of being in the wrong with ourselves and our fellows cannot be cured as long as we remain in the wrong with God.[11]

Very often it is assumed that the reason young people reject the Christian faith is because it is irrelevant, or because there is not enough scientific evidence to prove the existence of God, or perhaps because it is too difficult to accept that there is a God in the light of human suffering and evil. While each of these perspectives may have a certain amount of influence upon a person's rejection of God, none of these reasons get to the root issue. The root issue of unbelief is human rebellion against God. On one occasion I was discussing the attitudes of society towards Christianity with a group of young people. I decided to ask each of the young people what their immediate reaction to the word 'Christianity' was. One girl's answer was priceless: 'Ridiculous! Who is God to tell me what to do?'

This girl's answer powerfully affected me in two ways, firstly it was an example of raw honesty; secondly it confirmed the teaching of the Bible in regards to why people reject God. At the heart of our unbelief is our rebellion against God. Young people are no different from the rest of humanity; they don't want God because they don't want to give up the right to rule their own lives. This is the real problem with youth evangelism; it does not get to the root issue: human rebellion against God. It

---

[11]Packer, 214.

gives the impression that young people can come to Jesus while clinging to their idols, the greatest idol being love of self.

The heart of the Gospel

It is almost impossible to provide an adequate *summary* of the gospel. As soon as we think we have said it, we are brought to the realisation that there is so much more to be said. However, while we might not be able to exhaust the heights, depths, width and breadth of the gospel, we can go higher and deeper in our understanding, experience and communication of the gospel. In fact, the present situation demands that we do, because in most modern youth ministry contexts we are not even scratching the surface of the biblical gospel. We may not be able to exhaust the gospel, but we can get to the core of the gospel, Packer again helps us by demonstrating the heart of the gospel:

> The gospel tells us that our Creator has become our Redeemer. It announces that the Son of God has become man 'for us men and for our salvation' and has died on the cross to save us from eternal judgment. The basic description of the saving death of Christ in the Bible is propitiation, that is, as that which quenched God's wrath against us by obliterating our sins from his sight. God's wrath is his righteousness reacting against unrighteousness; it shows itself in retributive justice. But Jesus Christ has shielded us from the nightmare prospect of retributive justice by becoming our representative substitute, in obedience to his Father's will, and receiving the wages of our sin in our place.
>
> By this means justice has been done, for the sins of all that will ever be pardoned were judged and punished in the person of God the Son, and it is on

this basis that pardon is now offered to us offenders. Redeeming love and retributive justice joined hands, so to speak, at Calvary, for there God showed himself to be 'just, and the justifier of him that hath faith in Jesus.'

Do you understand this? If you do, you are now seeing to the very heart of the Christian gospel. No version of that message goes deeper than that which declares man's root problem before God to be his sin, which evokes wrath, and God's basic provision for man to be propitiation, which out of wrath brings peace.[12]

Redemption, reconciliation and propitiation are at the heart of the gospel. Some youth work and ministry contexts are happy to speak of the gospel in terms of redemption and reconciliation but very few are comfortable with propitiation. However, as Packer demonstrates, 'The *basic description* of the saving death of Christ in the Bible is propitiation.' In other words, we need to understand redemption and reconciliation in the light of propitiation. We need to be reconciled with God because we are rebels who are guilty of high treason; we have become God's enemies. God in his mercy has chosen to redeem sinners by offering his own son as a sacrifice: Jesus is the sacrifice who stands in our place and absorbs the righteous wrath of an all-powerful and holy God.

Perhaps we need to reflect on Packer's question: 'Do you understand this?' We can only touch the lives of young people with the gospel, if the gospel has first touched us. Have we felt both the piercing and pardoning which come from a true glimpse of the cross? Once we see the glory of the cross we can never settle for the superficial. May we be captured

---

[12] Packer, 212-213.

by the glory of the cross and may we be used of the Lord to draw others to it. The true gospel is radical, and if it is allowed to become central, it will bring the needed reformation to both youth work and youth ministry approaches to evangelism.

2 Regeneration for a New Generation

The 'Big Event' is a common characteristic of youth ministry. The programme usually follows a popular pattern. The first part of the event is similar to a concert, sometimes there will be some audience interaction, then someone will take to the stage and deliver a talk which in turn leads to what churches have traditionally referred to as the 'altar call'. At this point in the meeting, young people will be encouraged to respond to the message by repeating a prayer which indicates they want to commit their life to Christ; or they will be asked to raise their hand; or walk to the front of the platform to receive prayer or speak to a counsellor. Sometimes the response involves a combination of all four.

I've attended these events as a young Christian, I've also been involved in the planning of them, and I have spoken at them. At every level of involvement, from participant to speaker, I have always felt uneasy about the whole process. As a young person I struggled with the sense that something was missing; as a youth worker I had doubts about the authenticity of the conversions; and as a Bible teacher and preacher I now question the biblical basis of the methodology. The passing of time has only confirmed my doubts; in my time as a youth worker, I witnessed quite a number of the young people I was working with respond to invitations at events; on the surface it all looked very good. But the tragic fact is that many of the young people fell away in less than twelve months.

In the previous chapter, I identified ways in which the message is often misrepresented at youth ministry events; but this is not the only issue in youth evangelism, there are also problems with *the way* in which young people are being called to respond to the invitation to follow Christ. Youth ministries have understood the importance of 'conversion' to some extent and therefore tend to be more evangelistically minded than professional Christian youth work practitioners; however, while youth ministries have been more zealous in calling young people to follow Jesus, it is precisely at this point youth ministry falls into difficulty. John Piper powerfully illustrates this:

> I sometimes fear that we have so redefined conversion in terms of human decisions and have so removed any necessity of the experience of God's Spirit, that many people think they are saved when in fact they only have Christian ideas in their head, and not spiritual power in their heart.[13]

This is exactly what has happened with many youth ministry approaches to evangelism. Many leaders involved in youth ministry may have remained faithful to the distinct aim of the Christian faith (to call people to follow Jesus) but they have adopted the wrong methods. They have focused on the end result (profession of faith) and have not understood the importance of the process (gospel proclamation and the Holy Spirit's power). Those who adopt this approach have not realised

---

[13] John Piper, "How to Receive the Gift of the Holy Spirit", *Desiring God,* http://www.desiringgod.org/sermons/how-to-receive-the-gift-of-the-holy-spirit (accessed 10th October 2003).

that true conversions are not measured by the number of hands raised by individuals but by the number of hearts touched by God's Spirit. Our success is not determined by numbers but by a faithful presentation of the gospel and a prayerful reliance on God's Spirit to make the message effective in young people's hearts and minds.

We've already explored the problems of gospel misrepresentation; however, even when there is enough truth being presented in youth evangelism, the methods employed in the altar call can often be counter-productive to true conversion. For example, after the highly charged musical performance and the motivating message has been presented, the young people are often pressurised into making a decision before they have really understood the implications or counted the cost. The consequences of confusing premature responses with genuine conversions are tragic. If, as youth leaders, we misunderstand the nature of true conversion; we will tend to assume that young people's responses to the message at youth events are the same thing as conversion to Christ. When this happens we cause young people to begin their life of faith on the wrong foundation. We give them false assurance. We set them up for spiritual ship wreck and failure.

This was a problem I encountered many times as a Christian youth worker. As a youth worker in a para-church context, I would often take the young people I was working with to evangelistic events which were being hosted by local churches. On one occasion I had brought about ten young people to a gospel meeting which was being hosted in a hotel restaurant. Many of the young people had been making professions of faith and others were just starting to express an interest in Christianity. One young guy, in his late teens, had been taking his time. He seemed to be really wrestling with the whole idea of becoming a Christian. This particular night the gospel message seemed to be relevant for him. The preacher preached from the text, 'You are not far from the kingdom of God.' (Mark 12:34) By the end of the message, the young person had clearly been affected by what had been spoken. There was an invitation to respond; I went with him as he went out to speak to someone from the ministry team. The guy from the ministry team asked *why* the young guy had come out for prayer, and upon hearing that he was wanting to respond to the gospel, the leader threw his hands in the air, shouted 'Hallelujah!', handed him a New Testament, embraced him in a bear hug and said 'Welcome to family of God.' My heart sank. Not only did the leader not counsel the seeker and if appropriate lead him in prayer and repentance, but (as if by magic) he declared him a Christian. This young person left the meeting with the false assurance of man but without the genuine assurance of the Spirit. In a few months' time, family hostility towards his involvement with Christian groups would cause him to withdraw from Christian activities.

The questionable evangelistic methods used in youth ministry contexts triggers important questions about the nature of what it means to become a Christian. Why do youth ministries witness so many young people who make professions of faith; perhaps even go through the waters of baptism, yet show very little spiritual fruit? Why do so many churches have young people who profess to be Christians yet who are also deeply in love with the world? Why do many of the young people who make decisions at evangelistic youth events fall away from church and faith shortly after their commitment to Christ?

Many youth ministries have wrestled with these questions and have tried to develop various strategies in order to provide a solution. At the turn of the millennium, in many youth ministry circles, there was a major emphasis on youth cell groups. It was assumed that the reason why so many young people were making decisions and then quickly falling away was because there was a lack of 'follow up' and discipleship. In order to correct this there was a major push to integrate the new converts into cell groups. These cell groups were small discipleship groups which were designed with the intention of growth. In the particular model that I was working with, the vision was to see young people become Christians; be established in the faith and the church; be 'discipled' then sent out to reach other young people and eventually lead their own cell groups.

While the cell group model helped our youth ministries become more outward looking, the cell revolution hasn't removed the problem at all. The reason for fruitlessness and high fall away rates is much deeper than lack of follow up and discipleship programmes. The main reason for fruitless young professing Christians and high fall away rates is that many have been 'converted' by the means of shallow messages and manufactured responses. Ultimately this comes down to a lack of understanding of the nature of true conversion among those who present the gospel message in youth ministry outreaches. This in many ways is not the fault of the youth leaders; they have inherited this approach from the evangelical churches in which they themselves belong to. The main problem with modern youth evangelism is that many modern youth evangelists don't realise that true conversion is not the effect of a new resolution but the result of regeneration.

Conversion to Christ is not turning over a new leaf; it is the implanting of new life. This new life is the very life of God, Jesus referred to it as the new birth. Regarding the new birth, RC Sproul says, 'The term *born again* is a popular synonym for the theological term *regenerate*.' There are two essential things we need to understand about regeneration: the first one is that regeneration is *how* someone becomes a Christian. If a person has not experienced regeneration, they are not a Christian. Jesus put it in the following terms while discussing the issue with the Pharisee Nicodemus: "Truly, truly, I say to you, unless one is born again he cannot see the kingdom of God." (John 3:3)

The second essential thing we need to understand about regeneration is that only God can produce the rebirth in a person's life. In his conversation with Jesus, Nicodemus, upon perceiving the importance of the new birth, asked Jesus 'How can a man be born when he is old?' (John 3:4) Jesus responded by saying: 'The wind blows where it wishes, and you hear its sound, but you do not know where it comes from or where it goes. So it is with everyone who is born of the Spirit.'" (John 3:8) In other words, regeneration is a sovereign work of the Spirit of God. RC Sproul powerfully demonstrates this principle:

> In short, regeneration is a sovereign work of God. In other words, God exercises His power and His authority over you in His time and His way to bring about the regeneration of your heart. I stress this because many people understand regeneration as merely an activity of moral persuasion whereby God

woos or entices us to change and to come in His direction. . . Regeneration is not just God standing apart from us and trying to persuade us to come to Him, but God coming inside of us. He invades the soul, because there has to be a substantive change in the heart before we can come to Christ. [14]

Sproul's unfolding of the doctrine of regeneration stands in sharp contrast to the theory and practice of evangelism found in many youth ministry contexts. One of the reasons for this is that many youth leaders attend churches which no longer emphasise the Bible's teaching on regeneration. Another reason for this is the loss of biblical imagery regarding the human condition. In other words, modern evangelicalism has lost sight of the depths of the human problem; consequently, misunderstandings of the human condition have led modern evangelists to offer superficial solutions to human suffering.

Most gospel appeals have adopted the 'God-shaped hole' imagery. The emphasis in this kind of appeal is the idea that people were created for a purpose and that purpose is to know God. In rejecting God, every person has a space in their life that only God can fill. Instead of looking to God for fulfilment, people turn instead to music, fun, leisure, sex, drugs, or anything that the world promises will bring us happiness. Consequently, youth ministry appeals tend to focus on the fulfilment and purpose that a relationship with Jesus can bring.

Of course, the 'God-shaped hole' theory is absolutely true, and young people need to hear this truth. Very often when these appeals are made, the

---

[14] R.C. Sproul, *What does it mean to be born again?*, (Grand Rapids Michigan: Reformation Trust Publishing, 2010), Kindle Edition.

message really resonates with young people. The real problem is not with what *is* being said in this type of appeal, the problem is with what is *not* being said. While loss of purpose resulting in lack of happiness is *one* consequence of the fall, the problem is much deeper and more serious than the need for satisfaction.

The Bible does not only describe the call to Christ as a transition from a state of discontent to a state of fulfilment; the Bible describes conversion as a transition from death to life. The person without Christ does not only need wholeness, the person without Christ needs to be raised from the dead. This is why regeneration (new birth) is something that God must do.

It is essential that our youth ministry is grounded in the truth of regeneration, but it is equally important that we do not draw wrong conclusions about the doctrine of regeneration. Some people will argue that if conversion is God's work then Christians do not play any part at all in the process of a person coming to faith in Christ. This misunderstanding of regeneration causes people to neglect or even despise the role of evangelism. This is the position taken by hyper Calvinists, but I have also found it among charismatics.

During my time as a youth ministry student, there was a local charismatic church which attracted a reasonable number of young students. The church secured an old shop front and converted it into a coffee bar outreach. By the time it was finished the place looked really slick. I often attended their weekly prayer meetings, but I soon discovered that the methods being employed in reaching students were counterproductive. There seemed to be an assumption that there could be evangelism-less conversions. On a weekly basis someone from the team would pray something along the lines of: 'Lord, let people meet with your Spirit without anyone saying a word.' This is a misunderstanding of regeneration; while the Holy Spirit alone brings about the work of regeneration, we have a part to play. I also noticed that the cafe provided an information leaflet outlining the church's core values; the leaflet said: 'We believe it does more good to talk to God about people, than to talk to people about God.' This is a false dichotomy, as Christian youth leaders, we need to be talking to God about young people and talking to young people about God.

Understanding how the Holy Spirit brings about the work of regeneration is essential for anyone who is involved in communicating the Christian faith. It is not only a teaching which is important for ministers, it is equally important for Christian youth workers and youth leaders. From the examples of youth evangelism that we have observed so far, it is clear that there are two pitfalls that Christian youth leaders can fall into regarding the teaching on regeneration. On the one hand we can emphasise conversion as a decision to such a point that we eclipse the fact that it is primarily a work of the Holy Spirit, but on the other hand, we can neglect the role of communicating the gospel, assuming that the Holy Spirit will do it without the Word of God. The Westminster Shorter Catechism is a great help in highlighting the dual role of the word *and* the Spirit in relation to the process of regeneration and conversion:

Q 89 How is the word made effectual to salvation?

A. The Spirit of God maketh the reading, but especially the preaching, of the word, an effectual means of convincing and converting sinners, and of building them up in holiness and comfort, through faith, unto salvation.

The contemporary youth worker may respond to the language of the catechism like a bull to a red rag. The document is written in archaic language, and at a first glance may seem completely irrelevant to the world of young people. However, the catechism is telling us something very important. It is helping us understand *how* people become Christians. The catechism is simply summarising the teaching of the Bible which informs us that the Holy Spirit causes the reading and hearing of the word of God to be effective in the hearts and minds of the hearers. In other words, as we are faithful in communicating the word of God to young people, the Holy Spirit will bring it to life for them.

Understanding the Bible's teaching on regeneration should be a liberating experience for youth workers and youth pastors. Understanding regeneration should clarify our calling: we are not called primarily to be successful; we are called, first and foremost, to be faithful. The obsession with success has driven us to be numbers-orientated, it has caused us to crave popularity and the approval of the crowds, and it has led us to place our confidence in gimmicks instead of the gospel.

Since it is the Word of God that the Holy Spirit uses to bring about regeneration, it is essential that youth leaders are actively involved in sharing the Word of God. Youth leaders are instruments in the hand of God. John Owen argues that those who are involved in evangelism need to understand regeneration because they are the means by which God brings about regeneration:

> The work of the Spirit in regeneration ought to be seriously considered by the preachers and hearers of the gospel. As to the former, there is a peculiar reason for their attention to it, for they are employed in the work itself by the Spirit of God, as instruments in effecting it.[15]

These quotes from the catechism and Owen are not just some out-dated opinion from a bygone era; they are accurate expositions of the timeless truths of scripture:

> For "everyone who calls on the name of the Lord will be saved." How then will they call on him in whom they have not believed? And how are they to believe in him of whom they have never heard? And how are they to hear without someone preaching? And how are they to preach unless they are sent? As it is written, "How beautiful are the feet of those who preach the good news!" . . . So faith comes from hearing, and hearing through the word of Christ. (Rom 10:13-17)

Youth Work and regeneration

On the basis of my own observations, I would say that youth ministry tends to demonstrate a misunderstanding of conversion, whereas youth work contexts often demonstrate a rejection of the teaching of regeneration. This is not a new problem; the puritan, John Owen highlighted that this was an issue in his day:

---

[15] John Owen, *The Holy Spirit: His Gifts and Power,* (Scotland: Christian Heritage Imprint by Christian Focus, 2004), 158.

Among all the doctrines of the gospel, there is none opposed with more violence and subtlety, than that of regeneration by the powerful operation of the Holy Spirit; so there is scarcely anything more despised in the world, than that any persons should profess their experience of it, or declare the way and manner in which it was wrought on themselves. The very mention of it is become a reproach, among some who call themselves Christians; and to plead an interest in this grace, is to forfeit a man's reputation with many who would be thought to be wise, and boast themselves to be rational.[16]

Owen is arguing that the teaching of regeneration either tends to be out rightly rejected or subtly undermined. This has been my own experience in youth work and youth ministry contexts. In youth ministry, the adoption of market techniques and stage craft has subtly obscured the teaching of regeneration; in youth work circles, I have tended to experience outright resistance towards the teaching. The lack of emphasis on evangelism and regeneration among professional youth workers is related to the secular theories of youth work. Informal educators have argued that 'Christian youth work is often accused of being pre-occupied with the conversion, rather than building self-reliance and maturity.'[17] In other words, Christian youth workers cannot be committed to encouraging young people to place their trust in Christ and at the same time encourage them to be self-autonomous thinkers. This is one of the reasons why professional Christian youth work does not make evangelism and communicating the

---

[16] Owen, 223.
[17] Pughe.

need for regeneration among young people a priority.

In my own youth work I have encountered resistance to communicating the gospel in a variety of youth work situations. On one occasion I was part of a team of youth work students who were responsible for the planning and delivery of a youth residential weekend. In one of my activities I had incorporated a movie clip, a contemporary song, some discussion and a short concluding gospel challenge. At the end of the session one of the team members approached me in an indignant manner and rebuked me for including a short formal talk in the programme. She made it clear that formal presentations of the gospel have no place in youth work contexts. Although this was just her personal opinion; it was perfectly consistent with the philosophy of informal education. However, if we are to be faithful to Christ's commission, we must be faithful in presenting the gospel to young people rather than just assuming that they will work it out for themselves.

Other arguments against explaining the need for regeneration to young people are presented in theological terms. During a workshop on youth evangelism, one Christian youth worker expressed his outrage at the very concept of calling church young people to place their trust in Christ. From his perspective they should be considered Christians until they prove otherwise by an explicit denial of the faith. This assumption that church young people are Christians, by virtue of their church connection is common in both youth work and youth ministry contexts.

The idea that young people are regenerate on the basis of church involvement has serious implications, not least for eternity but also for the life of discipleship. As mentioned earlier, many young people in churches often lack some of the essential marks of the Christian life. Since it is assumed that they are Christians, youth leaders often focus on the lack of fruit rather than the root problem. In other words, the young people are pressurised into becoming more passionate, more active and more committed to the Christian faith. However, this overlooks a very real possibility: perhaps the young people are being asked to manifest fruit that they *cannot* produce because they are not connected to the vine. If young people are not demonstrating *any* signs of spiritual fruit, perhaps the exhortation they need is not: 'Get growing!' but 'Get planted!'

The Gospel Call

Some will also argue that since conversion is the work of God's Spirit, it is not our role to call people to respond to the gospel. However, this is not what the Bible teaches, and it is not the argument that I am making in this chapter. The problem with modern evangelism is not the fact that young people are being invited to follow Christ; the problem is with *how* they are being invited to follow Christ.

The model of initiation into the Christian faith used in youth evangelism is built around the 'Prayer of commitment.' In other words, becoming a Christian is simply a matter of 'Asking Jesus into my heart.' or 'giving my life to Jesus.' This approach to becoming a Christian is vastly different to the response that the Bible teaches is required for conversion. If we compare the modern response with the response called for by the Old Testament prophets, Jesus and the apostles, we will see a vast gulf between biblical conversion and modern conversion.

John the Baptist's call for response

> In those days John the Baptist came preaching in the wilderness of Judea, "Repent, for the kingdom of heaven is at hand." (Matt 3:1-2)

Jesus' call for response

> From that time Jesus began to preach, saying, "Repent, for the kingdom of heaven is at hand." (Matt 4:17)

Apostles' call for response

> And Peter said to them, "Repent and be baptized every one of you in the name of Jesus Christ for the forgiveness of your sins, and you will receive the gift of the Holy Spirit. (Acts 2:38)

If we analyse youth ministry gospel presentations in the light of the Bible, one of the questions we will be faced with is, why is there almost no mention of repentance in youth evangelism? The main reason seems to be that repentance relates to sin, and sin is negative, whereas youth ministry focuses on the positive. International youth ministry conference speaker, Mike Pilavachi, argues that issues relating to sin (especially sexual sin) need to be rethought by those who seek to reach and disciple young people. According to Pilavachi, the church's teaching on sin and sexuality 'Ain't working'.[18] He claims, regarding

---

[18] Greg, Haslam, ed., *Preaching the Word,* (Lancaster, Sovereign World, 2006), 361.

the biblical teaching on sexual morality, that '50% percent of Christian young people, who love Jesus and are committed to following him, don't understand why we have such a problem with these issues.'[19] He further argues that 'We have got to change the way we approach our teaching on them.'[20] How does he suggest we do this? Pilavachi suggests, 'One way in which we can do this is by majoring on the positive rather than the negative.'[21] In other words, we should not identify examples of sin and their consequences; we should identify what is good and celebrate it. However, Pilavachi seems to be falling into the common trap of presenting a false dichotomy. Celebrating the good and exposing wickedness is not an 'either or', it is a 'both and', the gospel does both. Perhaps the reason why '50% of Christian young people' don't 'get it' when it comes to biblical sexual morality is because youth ministry has sold them a version of Christianity which is packaged in half-truths, spin and euphemisms.

Pilavachi's comments are insightful in helping us understand one of the reasons why repentance is not a focus of youth ministry. From Pilavachi's perspective, the values of secular culture are too far removed from the values of the Bible; therefore, if we are going to connect with youth culture, we need to tone it down. However, we need to ask the question, is this helpful in the long run? Is this helping us to connect with non-Christian culture or is this non-Christian culture reshaping Christian values? I would argue it is the latter.

---

[19] Haslam. 361.
[20] Haslam. 361.
[21] Haslam, 361.

There are other reasons why repentance is not mentioned in youth ministry messages. The reasons for omitting issues relating to sin and repentance are not just cultural, they are stylistic. Thinking back to the big event, (which is where most youth evangelism altar calls take place), this event is based on an entertainment model: the performance. In order for an entertainment event to be successful it needs to be exciting, hyped and buzzing with a positive vibe. The big event is a celebration: it is festive; therefore, introducing topics such as sin, judgement and repentance into the big event is guaranteed to spoil the party and dampen the atmosphere. As one 22-year old student perceptively said, 'No one will listen to a preacher at a rave.'

One of the greatest challenges for the big event approach to evangelism is that the performance model incorporates competing factors into its programme. Sometimes the gospel does make an impact in these environments, but the emotional appeal, along with the music and the hyped up atmosphere, can actually conflict with the work of God's Spirit. Regarding the work of the Holy Spirit in bringing people to Christ, Jesus said: 'And when he comes, he will convict the world concerning sin and righteousness and judgement.' (John 16:8) Big event outreaches often short-circuit the good they do through contradictory actions. On the one hand, leaders will bring a message which they hope will challenge and convert, but on the other hand, they are so afraid of saying anything negative or convicting that might reduce the euphoric atmosphere which they have worked so hard to create.

One of the worst examples of this I ever witnessed was at a Christian youth music festival.

Each night included an impressive line-up of bands, and the message was to be delivered by a popular youth conference speaker and music artist. I was no longer in full-time youth work at this point, but given my background, I had been asked to be a counsellor in order to assist any young people who wanted to respond to the message.

The night was buzzing, the bands were a mixture; some very good and some not so good. The turnout was okay; there were perhaps about 100 people at the event. The time arrived, the music faded, the speaker delivered his animated talk and it was time to draw in the nets. It was time to call young people to respond to the message. This guy was quite innovative; rather than asking only the young people who were not Christians to pray a prayer of commitment, he just led the whole crowd in a prayer of commitment. He then asked if there was anyone who had prayed that prayer for the first time. The room went quiet as almost every hand in the room was raised (even some professing Christians had their hands raised). As the last hand was raised, the silence was broken as the speaker shouted, 'C'mon! Give yourselves a round of applause!' The room erupted, the band started up and it was back to party time. At some point in the course of events, it was mentioned that the ominous-looking adults wearing the high visibility jackets were there to speak to anyone who had made a commitment. No one approached the ministry team and there was no evidence that anyone had experienced a life-changing encounter with Jesus Christ.

The music was good, the message had just enough gospel content, but the invitation was a mockery. This experience confirmed to me that youth ministry is becoming more and more of a parody. That night I pretty much resolved that I would no longer be involved in this type of evangelism. I am sure that the ministries involved in this type of approach are sincere. I am also convinced that they are not intending to undermine the work of the gospel, but that is exactly what these methods do. The theme of this chapter is regeneration and conversion. An understanding of the conflicting nature of a hyped up crowd and the convicting ministry of the Holy Spirit is essential if we want to see young people genuinely respond to the gospel. If youth ministries are serious about seeing young people saved, and they want to continue to use the big event model, they need to be brave enough to allow space for silence and seriousness. They need to be so surrendered to the Lord that they are willing for the Holy Spirit to gate crash the party.

A.W Tozer touches on the issues surrounding genuine regeneration, conversion and repentance in the following statement:

> I consider it a good sign that some people are still asking questions like these in our churches: "What should happen in a genuine conversion to Christ?" and "What should a man or woman feel in the transaction of the new birth?" If I am asked, my answer is this: "There ought to be a real and genuine cry of pain!" That is why I am not impressed with the kind of evangelism that tries to invite people into the fellowship of God by signing a card. There should be a birth within, a birth from above. There should be the terror of seeing ourselves in violent contrast to the holy, holy God! Unless we come into this place of conviction and pain concerning our sin, I am not sure how deep and real our repentance will ever be. The man whom God will use must be undone, humble and

pliable. He must be, like the astonished Isaiah, a man who has seen the King in His beauty![22]

The call to reach young people with the gospel is just as urgent as it ever was. The battle for their souls is very real. Many like David have stepped up to join the battle hoping to win a generation for Christ, but they are weighed down with cultural baggage in the same way that David was weighed down with Saul's armour. There is a great need to rediscover God's weapons for reaching the world. Instead of seeing a generation of young people baptised in the Spirit of God we have seen ministries of the church baptised in the spirit of the world. As youth leaders we like to see ourselves as inheritors of a legacy of trail blazers and pioneers; yet too often Christian youth ministry simply reflects the culture of the day instead of challenging it. When youth ministry adopts the values and attitudes of secular society, it becomes the purveyor of the status quo rather than a prophetic voice for the kingdom of God.

Let us retrace the ancient paths and follow in the steps of John the Baptist, Jesus, the apostles; and men like Owen and Tozer. It has been said that: 'Tozer was often the voice of God when the words of others were but echoes.' In the midst of the contemporary confusion and compromise, there is a need for youth ministries that bear the mark of men like Owen and Tozer. There is a great need for the rediscovery of regeneration for a new generation.

---

[22] AW Tozer, "Conviction and Pain", *The Alliance,* http://www.cmalliance.org/devotions/tozer?id=207 (accessed 13 March 2014).

3 The Heart of Worship

For a number of decades, one of the major tensions in the church has been the area of worship. 'Worship Wars' have divided many local churches and denominations and the battle rages fiercely to this day. If traditional worship and liturgy are at one end of the spectrum, youth work and ministry approaches to worship are definitely at the other end. In contrast to the continuity and tradition of the more established churches, youth work and ministry have opted for worship expressions that are creative, interactive, entertaining and visual. Youth worker, and youth work lecturer, Ken Wilson describes the variety of worship he has encountered during his own youth work career which has spanned a number of decades:

> Through the years in my youth ministry I've been familiar with a considerable variety of worship styles and church experiments from the rave scene to the contemplative service; through times where the visual arts spoke louder than words; through millennial music styles, through silence; through story and testimony; through poetry and preaching.[23]

This eclectic collection of worship experiments is certainly characteristic of Christian youth work. The main reason for such a varied collection of worship styles is largely due to the ever-increasing

---

[23] Kenny Wilson, *Young People! Who Needs Them?*, (Cambridge: YTC Press, 2009), 134.

sub-cultures which young people identify themselves with. Youth workers have often argued that the worship style of traditional church represents a barrier to young people who identify more closely with the musical genres of secular culture.

In order to reach the various sub-cultures, youth workers have attempted to design worship formats that will appeal to individual groups. This approach to worship emphasises the importance of cultural expression. When it comes to designing services that will appeal to the various expressions of youth culture, I have found that Christian youth work has often been more innovative and creative, whereas youth ministry has adopted the contemporary Christian music worship style. Youth ministry events usually include contemporary praise and worship artists; or Christian rock bands, or more recently: emerging Christian rap and hip hop artists.

While the styles of worship expressed in youth work and youth ministry scenes may vary, they are often marked by the same ethos and characteristics. The worship tends to be individualistic, subjective and marked by an attitude of anti-tradition. This is in contrast to traditional worship, which would be characteristically collective in its expression; objective in its focus (word and sacrament); and respectful of tradition (sacrament, creed, liturgy and scripture reading).

I first encountered the subjective approach to worship during my first few years as a youth worker; when a fellow youth worker was sharing an innovative worship approach he had developed. The young people he was working with did not attend church and there was very little or no Christian influence in their lives. As a Christian youth worker, he understood his role in terms of helping young people develop physically, intellectually, emotionally, socially and *spiritually*. He felt that their culture placed them in a situation which was too far removed from the culture of the church, so he devised a strategy that would help them engage with worship. He designed an activity were the young people were encouraged to worship God as they imagined him to be. Whatever concept they had of God: that is how they were to approach him and engage with him. In other words, they were to worship whatever image they associated with God. While this approach to exploring spirituality is compatible with the relativistic principles of youth work, it is incompatible with the Christian faith; in fact, it is idolatry. True worship is in 'Spirit and truth', only those who are born again can worship God, and those who worship God must worship God as He is revealed through the Bible. When we worship a god of our own understanding, we no longer worship the God who made us in his image; we worship a god made in our own image. True worship is a response to the objective truth about God as revealed in the Word of God.

I have also found that the individualistic nature of youth work approaches to worship has manifested itself in a variety of different ways. On one occasion, I took a team of young people to an international youth event in Eastern Europe. The festival had a multitude of marquees, all dedicated to various causes. There were a few 'Worship Tents', and one in particular had various stations which individuals could work their way through, stopping and reflecting at each one. At one station there was a wooden cross and some nails; at another station there was a Nelson Mandela quote; and (the one that really got to me) a fountain and a pitcher of water where individuals could baptise themselves! Such approaches to worship reveal not only hyper-individualism but a vast disconnect with the church: a spirituality which is severed from the community of God's people.

The individualistic emphasis of youth work approaches was further brought home during a workshop on worship. A youth worker was leading the session and he was seeking to explain worship from a Christian perspective. The youth worker did an excellent job of demonstrating that people were created for worship; he did an outstanding job of illustrating the fact that people will always worship something. He effectively identified modern 'gods' such as sports, music, video games, etc. However, when he began to explain worship from a Christian perspective, there was a major disconnect from the historic Christian faith. He spoke about worship in terms of experience. He spoke about being in church and at times having 'amazing experiences' but at other times having very 'poor experiences'. He then said that for him, worship was at its best when he was alone, out in nature, playing a musical instrument or engaging in extreme sports. Of course, for Christians, there is a sense in which all that we do should be considered an act of worship, but this individualistic understanding of worship seriously misses the essence of biblical worship which is collective, and rooted in word and sacrament.

Underpinning the creative approaches of Christian youth work and the contemporary model of worship adopted by youth ministry is a negative attitude towards traditional worship styles. The following words were posted on a new young Christian's social network page after he started going to a contemporary church which was modelled on the worship style of Hillsong Australia: 'Grab the hymn book, scrunch it into a ball and volley it through the stain glass window: this is church but not as you know it!' I was amazed at how a brand-new Christian was able to capture the spirit of the contemporary approach to worship. This is part of the problem with the worship wars; it is not just that contemporary worship is an emerging cultural expression of worship; it is the fact that it is often wrapped in *anti*-traditional packaging. A further example of this is demonstrated by Wilson, who argues that traditional churches have contributed to the alienation of young people:

> We have to face the reality that young people are increasingly abandoning traditional church. Some young people see it is irrelevant because it just doesn't address their needs or circumstances; others leave because they feel left out; others feel that they have no meaningful connection to the adult congregation; others drift with the flow of culture and, if their interest is not engaged, gradually they lose interest.[24]

In other words, young people are abandoning (traditional) church because it's not all about them. It's not about their needs, their interests, and their sense of connectedness. Wilson argues that the church needs to move away from models of worship which discriminate against young people and develop models which are inclusive of the preferences of young people. He praises churches in the UK which are beginning to move away from having two standard Sunday services in favour of a more 'Interesting and innovative approach.' Notice

---

[24] Wilson, 134.

the words 'interesting and innovative'; in other words, churches which, in an attempt to attract the youth back to church, seek to offer young people what they want. Wilson argues that these churches which are developing innovative approaches to worship, are leading the way in regards to reducing the marginalisation of young people:

> Where there are open attitudes and willing hearts to church growth and experience, there are real signs of hope 'emerging.' As that rebalancing occurs, young people, who are alienated by the more traditional service and feel much more at home within the contemporary scene, are increasingly able to use their gifts and talents in such contexts. Where this happens, and young people again feel included rather than alienated, they are once again bringing life back into the church.[25]

Pete Ward also argues that churches need to make room for the variety of needs and interests of individual young people:

> What we need in our churches is a new sense of experimentation and freedom. If we are really going to reach out to different kinds of people then we need to allow these people to find the space within our churches to express their faith in their own way.[26]

There are number of major issues with the suggestions that Wilson and Ward are making. Aside from the anti-traditional bias, there is a hyper-individualism which strikes at the very essence of true worship. Ward argues that churches need to allow sub-cultures to express '*their* faith.'

---

[25] Wilson, 135.

[26] Ward, 177.

However, when it comes to cultures and sub-cultures and collective worship, there is no such thing as *'their* faith', there is only *the* faith. Jude speaks of 'The faith that was once for all delivered to the saints.' (Jude 1:3) In other words, the Christian faith is objective, universal and historical. God invites all peoples and cultures to come and partake of *the* faith; therefore, speaking of cultural varieties of faith is completely misleading. Further, subcultures are not called to express *their* faith in *'their own* way' but *the* Faith in *God's* way. The Westminster Confession demonstrates this effectively:

> The acceptable way of worshipping the true God is instituted by himself, and so limited by his own revealed will, that he may not be worshipped according to the imaginations and devices of men, or the suggestions of Satan, under any visible representation, or any other way not prescribed in the holy Scripture" (WCF 21.1).

In other words, true worship is not about *my* creativity, or *my* preferred music genre or *my* personal preferences; true worship is about God's preferences. Worship is not all about me, it's all about God. The real problem with the claims and suggestions made by Ward and Wilson and other advocates of culture-defined worship is that they turn the sanctuary into a market place. They build their methodology on market driven strategies and instead of making Christian converts, they produce Christianised consumers. To be sure, their argument for worship based on cultural relevance does lead to authentic cultural expression: the cultural expression of a consumerist society which worships at the altar of 'Me'.

Carl Trueman, in his book *The Creedal Imperative,* offers some good insight into the negative influence of consumerism upon church life and worship:

> The impact of consumerism is one reason why church sessions and elder boards often spend more time than is decent on discussions about worship and programs. Someone will make the point that certain young people have left because the worship is not to their liking and thus the church needs to think again about how it does things. Laying aside the fact that, for most of us, no church gives us everything we want in worship but we are nonetheless happy to attend because the Word is truly preached, it is interesting to note the session member's response: we need to do something, to think again about worship. In other words, we need to respond to the needs of the consumer. An alternative approach might be that we need to do a better job of explaining why we do what we do, and what the obligations entailed in solemn vows of membership are; yet this is often not the knee-jerk reaction to such concerns. The consumer-is-king mentality renders all established and time-tested practices unstable and utterly negotiable.[27]

Trueman is warning against the fickleness of traditional churches revamping their services in order to cater to the fleeting fads of society. He instead argues that the church needs to understand who it is, why it exists, and then communicate this with clarity and conviction.

Does this mean that culture is not important? Not at all. Trueman sheds further light:

---

[27] Carl Trueman, *The Creedal Imperative*, (Wheaton IL, Crossway, 2012), Kindle edition.

It is obvious that worship services must have some connection to the wider culture (language, location, etc.), but no biblical writer expends any real energy reflecting on contextualization. It would seem that such matters have produced a veritable industry in the modern church world but were very low on the list of the New Testament writer's priorities, possibly because they regarded them as of minimal importance and matters of mere common sense.[28]

In other words, Christian youth work and youth ministry have invested an awful lot of time and energy in an area that the Bible does not prioritise. They have inflated the importance of secondary cultural issues and in the process have created a market for themselves. Richard Davies has also identified this fact: 'In Christian youth work we have created a market out of young people who need deinstitutionalised services, rather than seeking to help young people live out their faith in a godly intergenerational community.' In other words, focusing on issues surrounding cultural expression has helped youth work build up an industry for itself but it has utterly failed in terms of integrating young people into the inter-generational community of God's people.

The development of youth ministry approaches and contemporary worship styles with an anti-traditional bias has had a number of negative consequences. One of these consequences is that it can create dissatisfaction with a more established model of church among young people who do attend more 'traditional' churches. By traditional, I am not just thinking about high Anglican, or Presbyterian, I am even thinking of charismatic and Pentecostal churches. For example, a Pentecostal

---

[28] Trueman.

church I know of had developed a large and growing youth ministry. Along with sports activities and youth cafés, it also hosted regular contemporary Christian music festivals. After a short period of time, the youth within the church became more and more disillusioned with the regular church services. Eventually some of them stopped going to church altogether.

Another consequence of the anti-traditional experimental approach is the generational division that it creates within local churches. Not only does it create inter-generational division, but in contrast to what Wilson was saying earlier, it can actually lead to the marginalisation of older believers. I have observed this in at least two different local churches. In both situations, the churches had called a younger pastor; the younger pastors surrounded themselves with younger leaders (peers), and older leaders and longstanding members were pushed to the outskirts. In both cases the agenda was very similar, the younger leadership wanted to take the church through a transition in order to appeal to a contemporary audience.

Closely related to the anti-tradition and consumerist approach to youth ministry and worship is the obsession with innovation. In order to get young people to buy into whatever brand of youth work and ministry is being peddled, it needs to be 'relevant'; in order to maintain relevance, youth work and ministry needs to have an emphasis on innovation. Andy Hawthorne, founder of the Message Trust, emphasises the importance of innovation (which is defined as, 'The act of introducing something new.'). Hawthorne argues:

Unfortunately the church has a habit of getting stuck in a rut. Four hundred years ago roughly, religion and institution had replaced revival and inspiration. From the fires of Jerusalem, the church had gone cold. So the Reformation took place, an amazing time in church history when innovators dragged the church kicking and screaming back to where it needed to be. Their motto was 'semper reformanda', 'always to be reformed' – in other words, holding to scripture truth but always looking to creatively interpret it in language people could understand. Of course, one by one, the reformers got burned at the stake. So 400 years later, lots of the church is still using their prayer book. Somewhere in heaven, Cranmer is holding his head in his hands, crying, 'Duh! Don't you realise that book wasn't meant to be for 400 years!?'[29]

Hawthorne is actually presenting a revisionist view of history. His interpretation of 'Semper Reformanda' is misleading; from his point of view, it means *always changing*, from the reformers' point of view, it meant *always being faithful to scripture*. This is the major difference between the reformers (whose example Hawthorne believes he is following) and youth ministries which pursue innovation. Innovators are driven by the ever changing winds of culture; reformers resist the winds and waves of human ingenuity (which seek to redefine revelation) by holding fast to the immovable rock of apostolic tradition: the scriptures.

Not only does Hawthorne demonstrate a misunderstanding of 'Semper Reformanda', he seems to misunderstand the nature and purpose of the Anglican prayer book. His hypothetical

---

[29] Andy Hawthorne, "Ideas that Change the World", *The Message,* http://www.message.org.uk/ideas-that-change-the-world/ (accessed 9th November 2013).

caricature of Cranmer despairing over the preservation of the prayer book could not be further from the truth. The men who developed the creeds, confessions and liturgy of the church – be they Anglican, Presbyterian or otherwise – were not primarily driven by the need for innovation and diversity, they were motivated by the need for preservation and unity. I'm not an Anglican, so I'll let John Stott respond to Hawthorne:

> The Church of England is a liturgical church. It has a Book of Common Prayer, and a Common Worship service book . . . Some say that set services inhibit spontaneity and the freedom of the Spirit. This does not have to be the case. Form and Freedom are not necessarily incompatible with one another . . . Why should we value liturgy? First, there is plenty of biblical warrant for liturgical forms . . . Secondly, a liturgy enshrines truth and safe-guards uniformity of doctrine. Thirdly, it gives a sense of solidarity both with the past and with the rest of the church in the present. Fourthly, it protects the church from idiosyncrasies of the clergy. These are great gains. They make me thankful that the Church of England is a liturgical church.[30]

Stott's four arguments for the role of liturgy, (or creeds and confessions), are the keys to safeguarding the very things that are being lost in many Christian youth work and youth ministry approaches to worship. Liturgy, creeds and confessions help preserve the biblical nature of worship; they help preserve truth and unity; they help the church remain connected to the church of the past and the wider church of the present; and

---

[30] John Stott, *The Living Church: Convictions of a Life Long Pastor* (England: IVP, 2007), 170.

they protect the church from being dominated by personality cults. Yet these four areas are the very areas where Christian youth work and ministry are failing. The reason for this is that they have sacrificed the preservation of apostolic tradition for the innovation of cultural expression.

A lot of the confusion surrounding cultural issues could be clarified through understanding what reformed believers have referred to as the regulative principle. The regulative principle relates to the section of the Westminster Confession of Faith which we explored earlier:

> The acceptable way of worshipping the true God is instituted by himself, and so limited by his own revealed will, that he may not be worshipped according to the imaginations and devices of men, or the suggestions of Satan, under any visible representation, or any other way not prescribed in the holy Scripture" (WCF 21.1).

In connection with the regulative principle, reformed believers have distinguished between the *elements* of worship and the *circumstances* of worship:

> Elements of worship are areas such as the reading and preaching of Scripture; the administration of the sacraments of baptism and the Lord's Supper; the presentation of offerings; the singing of psalms and hymns; and, sometimes, the taking of oaths. . . Circumstances of worship are things that are necessary for an element to be done. Thus, for example, an element of worship is the singing of psalms and hymns, but a circumstance could be that this singing is accompanied by an accordion and a banjo. Again, an element in worship is that the reading and preaching of God's Word should occur on the Lord's Day; a circumstance is that it should

happen at ten thirty on Sunday morning instead of two o'clock on Sunday afternoon.[31]

Understanding the difference between the elements of worship and the circumstances of worship is essential because it helps clear away a lot of the smoke which surrounds the cultural expression debate. It places a lot of the 'cultural' issues raised in Christian youth work circles in their proper place. In other words, true worship is about something greater than style. Lucas argues that:

> True: gospel-driven, biblical, and Reformed worship transcends style; it can be expressed in a variety of local churches through a variety of valid expressions.[32]

Consequently, worshippers are bound together by something far greater than consumerist driven sub-cultures. Lucas argues further that:

> There are common, gospel-driven, biblical principles that hold our worship together - whether we are part of a traditional, middle class, rural congregation; a multinational, multiracial, urban congregation; or a non-traditional, contemporary, suburban congregation.[33]

In other words, when our worship is gospel-centred, superficial cultural differences are eclipsed by the unity that flows from a focus on the glory of Christ.

---

[31] Sean, Michael, Lucas, *Being Presbyterian*, (Philipsburg, New Jersey: P&R Publishing Company, 2006), Kindle.

[32] Lucas.

[33] Lucas.

A gospel-centred approach to worship will help divert our focus from superficiality to substance; it will deliver us from being people-centred and empower us to be God-centred. Lucas again demonstrates how gospel centeredness helps us transcend the issues surrounding style:

> Whether we sing Bach or rock is relatively unimportant compared to the much greater need that we have to hear God speak to us by his Word, to recall God's promises made to us in Christ, to be reminded of the gospel in Word and sacrament, and to be transformed by the Spirit using his Word in our lives.[34]

The pre-eminence of Christ over style is powerfully demonstrated in a story that was told by contemporary song writer and worship leader, Matt Redman. He tells the story of how his pastor once did something very radical. Although their church seemed to be leading the way in a cutting edge contemporary worship style, the pastor sensed that they were missing the heart of worship. At the height of contemporary success, he told the church: 'We just need to strip everything away to check where our hearts are in worship.' The pastor had perceived that the form of worship was eclipsing the heart of worship. Consequently they laid aside the instruments and there was no sound system for a period of time. It was at that time Matt Redman wrote the popular worship song called 'The Heart of Worship.'

The background to the song 'The Heart of Worship' is powerful, it is a brilliant illustration of how focusing on *the style* of worship can take us away from *the heart* of worship. It is encouraging to

---

[34] Lucas.

hear contemporary worship leaders, like Redman, emphasise the nature of true worship. Redman is clear that Worship *is not* about the form (instruments and style can get actually get in the way); worship *is* about the condition of our heart. Worship is not about the rhythm of the music because worship is ultimately all about Jesus.

Sadly, modern worship leaders and young Christians have adopted (and developed) Matt Redman's style of worship but not his heart of worship. I remember gathering in the college chapel one day, and on one side of me there was a theology student and on the other side a youth work student. As we were waiting for the service to start, the youth work student groaned, 'Aww, man, I can't stand these old hymns.' The theology student and I looked at each other and then attempted to explain to him the power and significance of the hymns of the church. The youth work student stared blankly at us, and replied, 'Man, you guys just don't understand my culture.' This was quite amusing because the theology student and I were only a few years older than he was, but not only that, the theology student looked like a member of a death metal band, complete with shaved head, spikey goatee and outrageous-looking biker boots. We were not as far removed from his culture as he thought, but I'm sure the irony was lost on him.

At the risk of being misunderstood, I am not arguing against a contemporary style of worship. Music has always played an important part in my life, and I have worshiped in contemporary churches for most of my Christian life. However, I am highlighting the fact that many who are in the contemporary worship scene are losing sight of the nature of true worship.

What I hope these examples demonstrate is that when it comes to worship, youth ministries will often emphasise cultural expression at the expense of Christ exaltation. They have lost what Redman calls 'the heart of worship.' In an interview about the song, Matt Redman highlights this tendency within the contemporary worship scene:

> So often in our worship and in the church, we shrink God down. We make Him like He is one of us. You even hear songs that sound like they could be a normal love song or pop song. I know what people are trying to do. They are trying to be culturally relevant. But there is a bigger value in worship than cultural relevance – it's the glory of God. Let's write songs that paint a big picture of God. Let's have worship services that immerse us in God's splendour. Let's not shrink God down. We are the ones who are going to do the shrinking.[35]

Redman's words are powerful. Perhaps, as youth workers and youth leaders we can learn from Redman's message. Perhaps we need to do with our ministries what Redman's pastor did with the instruments and sound system. Perhaps we need to allow God to strip from us all that is non-essential and hindering God's true purposes in our lives and ministries. Perhaps we need to lay our agendas and assumptions about culture on the altar, and bow down and worship Jesus. As we catch a fresh glimpse of Jesus, we will burn the golden calves of cultural expression and discover the simplicity and power of Christ exaltation.

---

[35] Matt Redman, Interview by Laura J. Bagby, "Living Out of a 'Heart of Worship'", *CBN Music,* http://www.cbn.com/cbnmusic/interviews/bagby_mattredman0628 04.aspx (accessed 12 March 2013).

4 Need for Creed

What are the essential characteristics of *Christian* youth work? This is the question that was given to us as youth work students in our first term at the start of our BA course in youth work and applied theology. During the discussions that ensued, many diverse and interesting answers were put forward. The one that sticks in my mind was the suggestion that 'Christian youth work should be Bible-based'. Of course, I agreed with this wholeheartedly, but it was not long before I discovered that professional Christian youth work is anything but Bible-based.[36] However, studying youth work and theology in an evangelical, interdenominational theological college soon led me to discover another reason why the idea of a Bible-based approach to Christian youth work was problematic. No one could agree on what the Bible actually taught! This scenario is not an isolated incident; it is actually reflective of the wider evangelical movement. In this chapter we are going to consider the relationship between doctrine and historic evangelicalism; doctrine and modern evangelicalism; and doctrine and Christian youth work and ministry.

---

[36] Appendix: What's the Point?

Historic Evangelicalism

Over the years, as I have reflected on the doctrinal division and schismatic nature of evangelicalism, I have arrived at the realisation that evangelicalism is in its present condition largely due to the fact that it has drifted from the wider theological framework in which it initially emerged. Evangelicalism owes its beginnings to the reformation, and while the reformation was evangelical in nature, it was also confessional. In other words, the churches were bound together by a common confession. The Scottish Presbyterian creed has traditionally been the Westminster Confession; the Anglicans (as we have already touched upon) have the Book of Common Prayer and the Articles of Faith; and even some of the early Baptists were defined by the London Baptist Confession of Faith.

In spite of the confessional background to evangelicalism, later independent evangelicals were not as rigorous as their forebears in the area of church confessions, but they were nonetheless identified by a commitment to core doctrines. An example of the core doctrines, which marked early evangelicalism, can be seen in the historic Evangelical Alliance (EA) Statement of Faith:[37]

---

[37] Evangelical Alliance modified its statement of faith in 2005. However, since this discussion is about *historic* marks of evangelicalism, I have chosen to use the original statement in this chapter. While the new statement still bears many of the marks of traditional evangelicalism, it is a lot weaker in certain areas, e.g. they have dropped the term 'triune'; its statement of Sovereignty is not as strong; and it is not very clear on the nature of atonement (they have removed the phrase 'substitutionary'). Given the contemporary tendency to reject propitiation, this modified EA statement tends to

Evangelical Christians accept the revelation of the triune God given in the Scriptures of the Old and New Testaments and confess the historic faith of the Gospel therein set forth. They here assert doctrines which they regard as crucial to the understanding of the faith, and which should issue in mutual love, practical Christian service and evangelical concern.

* The sovereignty and grace of God the Father, God the Son and God the Holy Spirit in creation, providence, revelation, redemption and final judgement.

* The divine inspiration of the Holy Scripture and its consequent entire trustworthiness and supreme authority in all matters of faith and conduct.

* The universal sinfulness and guilt of fallen man, making him subject to God's wrath and condemnation.

* The substitutionary sacrifice of the incarnate Son of God as the sole all-sufficient ground of redemption from the guilt and power of sin, and from its eternal consequences.

* The justification of the sinner solely by the grace of God through faith in Christ crucified and risen from the dead.

* The illuminating, regenerating, indwelling and sanctifying work of God the Holy Spirit.

* The priesthood of all believers, who form the universal Church, the Body of which Christ is the

---

reflect the climate of the day rather than the historic teaching of evangelicalism.

Head and which is committed by His command to the proclamation of the Gospel throughout the world.

* The expectation of the personal, visible return of the Lord Jesus Christ in power and glory.[38]

The opening paragraph of the Statement of Faith stresses several essential convictions. Firstly, it declares that, 'Evangelical Christians accept the revelation of the triune God given in the Scriptures of the Old and New Testaments.' In other words, evangelicals base their understanding of God on the Bible, which they believe to be the 'revelation' of God. This means that God has made himself known through the words of Holy Scripture. Secondly, it declares that evangelicals, 'Confess the historic faith of the Gospel therein set forth.' In other words, their faith is not some novel innovative expression of Christianity; it is the historic gospel which was delivered to the apostles by Jesus Christ and by revelation of the Holy Spirit. Thirdly, they 'Assert doctrines which they regard as crucial to the understanding of the faith.' By this, they are declaring that the doctrines set forth in the statement are essential for understanding the Christian faith. If a person wants to understand Christianity, he must understand these doctrines. Fourthly, these doctrines should, 'Issue in mutual love, practical Christian service and evangelical concern.' In other words, the doctrines are not intended to be abstract theories which bear no practical relevance. They are the very means by which Christians will be motivated towards love, service and concern for people who are lost.

---

[38] Evangelical Alliance Statement of Faith (Old Version)

At this point it should be clear that early evangelicalism was primarily concerned with the knowledge of God as revealed in the Bible; a historical confession of faith; the importance of doctrine, practical Christian service and concern for the lost. For the evangelical, these areas were woven together and not one of them was considered dispensable. This is not the case within evangelicalism today. Consequently, it is not the case within Christian youth work and youth ministry. Liberal scholarship (biblical scholarship which rejects the inspiration and authority of scripture) has influenced many evangelical churches, leaders and Christians to the point where the Bible is no longer fully trusted; doctrine is not considered important; historical confessions are fossils of the past; and it is assumed that knowledge of God and practical Christian service can take place without the former 'baggage' of scripture, doctrine and historical confessions. The condition of the wider church has significant consequences for Christian youth work and ministry. In many places, the church is like a ship without a rudder; a house without a foundation; and a tree without roots. Consequently, many Christian youth workers and leaders are seeking to teach young people the Christian faith in church contexts where there is very little expression of the historic Christian faith.

Modern Evangelicalism

In recent years, one of the latest offshoots of evangelicalism has been the Emergent Church.[39]

---

[39] For a more detailed critique of the Emergent Church see Kevin DeYoung and Ted Cluck's *Why we're not emergent by two guys who should be.*

The Emergent Church is mainly known for its appeal to younger Christians; its innovative and creative worship experiments; its rejection of dogma, creeds and the belief that scripture is the final authority for faith and practice; and the embracing of postmodern values and attitudes, in particular moral and theological relativism.

Youth Worker, Stewart Cutler, in a series of blog articles, explored the similarities between Christian youth work and the Emergent Church and concluded that: 'Youth Work and the Emerging Church seem to share a value base.'[40] Stewart is correct in this assessment; at the heart of both Christian youth work and emergent expressions of the Christian faith is a commitment to relativism and a suspicion of authority structures.

The connection between liberalism, the emergent church and Christian youth work can clearly be seen in the following extract which was taken from an Urban Saints Youth Leader Training Resource. The document focuses on the relationship between youth work and Christian doctrine, it has been written by Phil Green, who draws heavily on the work of Rob Bell. While the following extract is quite lengthy, it helps further highlight the influence of emergent thinking upon Christian youth work theory and practice.

> The word 'doctrine' can be a rather daunting word, a subject that many consider dated and dull. It's certainly not a word that you are likely to put on your youth group publicity leaflet! However, Rob Bell's approach to the subject is anything but 'dated and dull' - he attempts to approach the subject in a fresh way and seeks to give doctrine a facelift.

---

[40]Stewart Cutler, http://stewartcutler.com/archives/1502 (accessed 24th September 2013)

It's about time someone did this. After all, a Christian doctrine is a summary statement explaining what Christians believe the Bible says about a particular topic. This means that exploring doctrine shouldn't be dull; it should be vibrant, dynamic and life changing.

Springs or Bricks?

Rob Bell encourages us to think of doctrines as being similar to the springs of a trampoline. The springs are crucial; however, they are not what it's all about - they simply hold the mat in place so the jumping can take place. He says, "The springs are statements and beliefs about our faith that help give words to the depth that we are experiencing in our jumping. I would call these doctrines of the Christian faith."

Rob Bell explains that the problem is often that doctrines are considered to be bricks rather than springs. He gets us to imagine each core doctrine of the Christian faith is represented by a brick, and together these bricks form a wall. He points out several problems with this idea.

How flexible are the springs?

Bricks are very set; they're not flexible, there can be no movement and if you begin to doubt or question one of the bricks there is a chance that the whole wall will collapse. You may be thinking that this isn't a problem; after all, doctrines don't need to be flexible because they are very set; after all, as it says In Malachi 3:6, "I the Lord do not change." At this point we need to remember that, in this illustration, the bricks and springs DO NOT represent the truth about God and who he is, which is unchanging, they represent our belief about God and our understanding of God - and this should be dynamic, it should be subject to change and development. That's one of the exciting things about being a Christian; we keep growing and developing in our understanding of God. God is surrounded by mystery; he reveals bits and pieces to us, but certainly not everything. Therefore, static bricks just aren't a good picture, dynamic springs are.[41]

Green thinks that Bell's approach is helpful in influencing Christian youth workers in the way they should approach teaching Christian doctrine. He also thinks that we can take a flexible approach to doctrine and that this will not have any impact on 'The truth about God.' On the contrary, Christian doctrines are expressions of the truths about God as they are revealed in scripture. Carl Trueman demonstrates the essential role of creeds in the following statement: 'Creeds and confessions are human attempts to summarise and express the basic elements of the Christian faith.'

Confessional Christianity

A creedal approach to Christian doctrine is the exact opposite to that which is endorsed by Bell and Green. The 'springs' metaphor may appeal to the contemporary mind-set because it paints a picture of a free and dynamic approach to doctrine, but in reality, it's a recipe for spiritual disaster. Trueman demonstrates further the nature of creeds and the consequences of rejecting biblical and historic confessions of faith:

---

[41] Phil Green, "Bell, Trampolines, Bricks and Youthwork: Leaders", *Urban Saints*
http://m.energize.uk.net/articles/belltrampolinesbricksandyouthwork (accessed 23rd September 2013).

Creeds and confessions are, in fact, necessary for the well-being of the church, and that churches that claim not to have them place themselves at a permanent disadvantage when it comes to holding fast to that form of sound words which was so precious to the aging Paul as he advised his young protégé, Timothy. . . The need for creeds and confessions is not just a practical imperative for the church but is also a biblical imperative.[42]

In other words, Trueman is arguing that creeds are not just beneficial for the church but they are essential for the church's health and wellbeing. He argues that creeds are the means by which the apostolic tradition is preserved. Without this preservation of apostolic tradition, the church is at the mercy of innovators who will lead the church according to their own imaginations and agendas. Trueman demonstrates further reasons why a creedal, and therefore non innovative, approach to doctrine is so important:

Creeds and confessions that have proved useful over the centuries are clearly immune to the passing fads and tastes of the present. They speak to issues that the church has found important for generations. . . A church with a creed or confession has a built-in gospel reality check. It is unlikely to become sidetracked by the peripheral issues of the passing moment; rather it will focus instead on the great theological categories that touch on matters of eternal significance.[43]

In contrast, to Bell and Green, Trueman shows several strong reasons for thinking of doctrine in terms of something that is solid and trustworthy.

---

[42] Trueman.

[43] Trueman.

The path we choose as Christian youth workers, in regards to how we approach doctrine, is incredibly important. Is our ministry marked by apostolic authority because it is grounded in apostolic revelation or are we being blown by the chaotic winds of relativism?

Green develops the anti-doctrine metaphor further:

> Another problem with brick walls is that they usually end up keeping some people in and other people out. If we are not careful we can quickly end up with a 'them' and 'us' mentality. The people who believe the same thing as us are 'in' and those who don't are 'out'. It's then the job of the 'in' people to bring the 'out' people inside the brick wall by convincing them to believe the same things they do. Just think for a moment about the way Jesus worked...it wasn't like this. He invited people to spend time with him and experience what was going on. Then they began to explore the 'doctrine' and decided whether they wanted to stay 'in'. In other words they came 'in' first, before they believed. [44]

It is easy to see what is driving Green's aversion to fixed doctrinal categories. He has understood that clear creedal convictions lead to the exclusion of those who reject them. However, he doesn't seem to understand that this is one of the primary functions of creedal formulations. Trueman, again demonstrates this: 'A confession is a positive statement of belief; but in making a positive statement of belief, it inevitably excludes those who disagree with its content.'[45]

---

[44] Green.
[45] Trueman.

Green argues that Jesus did not teach using exclusive categories. He claims that Jesus enabled people to 'belong before they believed'. I have no idea which 'Jesus' Green is talking about, but it is not the Jesus of the New Testament. Regarding Jesus, John the Baptist declared:

> I baptize you with water for repentance, but he who is coming after me is mightier than I, whose sandals I am not worthy to carry. He will baptize you with the Holy Spirit and fire. His winnowing fork is in his hand, and he will clear his threshing floor and gather his wheat into the barn, but the chaff he will burn with unquenchable fire. (Matt 3:11-12)

Jesus constantly divided people into categories. The sheep and the goats; the wheat and the chaff; and the righteous and the wicked are just three examples of the exclusivity of Christ's teaching. Why is it that many youth workers, like Green, represent a Jesus which is very different to the Jesus found within the pages of scripture? Why is it that so many Christian youth workers claim to be carrying out *Christian* youth work yet deny the very foundations of the Christian faith? Why is it that the New Testament places such a strong emphasis on the need to preserve true Christian teaching and doctrine yet Christian youth workers demonstrate a laissez–faire approach to doctrine? Trueman again, identifies the real reason:

> Religion, particularly traditional religion, finds itself at a cultural moment where it is feared because it dares to say that some beliefs and practices are true and good while others are false and bad.[46]

---

[46] Green.

In other words, the anti-doctrine attitude among many contemporary Christian youth workers is not a fruit of their faith; it is a consequence of their culture. It is a sign that they have not been transformed by the renewing of their minds, but have conformed to the pattern of the world. Of course many who take such anti-creedal approaches to their ministry do not always realise the true source of their own values and attitudes. Many, like Green, seem convinced that their innovative approach to Christian doctrine is actually modelled on the example of Jesus and the teaching of the Bible. Once again, Trueman highlights the deceptive nature of an anti-creedal attitude:

> It would be a tragic irony if the rejection of creeds and confessions by so many of those who sincerely wish to be biblically faithful turned out to be not an act of faithfulness but rather an unwitting capitulation to the spirit of the age.[47]

One of the real tragedies of the subtle way in which secular humanism has influenced the thinking of so many Christian youth workers is the negative affect it has on their ministries. The pressures of secularism seem to be too strong for many Christian youth workers to resist. This is observable in an example Green cites from his youth work practice:

> Last year I was taking a lesson, and as usual the young people were asking me questions and I was doing my best to defend the Christian faith. It then struck me that I might be doing more harm than good. I realised that there was a good chance that my

---

[47] Green.

'answers' were actually putting them off Christianity, not attracting them to it. It got me thinking. These young people needed to encounter Jesus FIRST.[48]

It sounds to me that Green, like so many Christian youth workers, began to doubt the good he was doing because it was not met with immediate approval, acceptance and success. Ministry among young people who are not Christians is hard work. You encounter strong negative attitudes and deep resistance to the gospel. Sadly, too many innovators have used this as an opportunity to introduce other approaches, approaches which they promise will bring more success. Of course, when you lay aside absolute truth claims, the cross, the warning of final judgement and the call to repentance and faith, and trade them in for relativism, entertainment and 'do it yourself philosophy': you *will* encounter less resistance, you *will* have more success, but you will also lose sight of your true calling which was to reach a lost generation with the everlasting gospel.

Not only does Green begin to doubt the good he might actually have been doing, he seems to completely reverse the process of conversion. He assumes that he can lead young people to encounter Christ without first proclaiming Christ. He is ultimately separating experience from truth; this is simply a further characteristic of postmodern thinking. Trueman also exposes this popular fallacy:

Separation of doctrine and Christian experience . . . [is] arguably, a species of liberalism . . . We tend not to see evangelicalism in terms of liberalism because of its public adherence to supernaturalism and our

---

[48] Green.

tendency to associate liberalism with varying degrees of antisupernaturalism. Yet we must remember that liberalism is not primarily a rejection of the supernatural; it is a reconfiguration of the nature of Christianity in such a way as to highlight religious psychology or experience and downplay or marginalize doctrine.[49]

Trueman's words may come as a shock to many evangelicals. Most evangelicals don't tend to associate liberalism with evangelicalism. Green is clearly seeking to evangelise, so how can it be claimed that he is demonstrating liberal thinking? Trueman is arguing that liberalism is not just about denying the miracles of Jesus. Liberalism, he argues, is the *separation of doctrine and Christian experience*. It is the *emphasis of experience* and the *setting aside of doctrine*. This is exactly what Bell promotes; it is the ideology that Green sets forth in his youth leader training document and it is the philosophy of many contemporary Christian youth workers. The tragedy in all of this is the fact that many youth workers are working hard evangelistically, but the message they are spreading is liberalism and not the historic Christian faith. The message being promoted by many Christian youth workers and youth leaders is simply a Christianised form of secular humanism.

The influence of Emergent philosophy within Christian youth work is further demonstrated by the following statement which was made by Tony Jones at a national youth workers convention.

Emergent doesn't have a position on absolute truth, or on anything for that matter. Do you show up at a dinner party with your neighbours and ask, 'What's

---

[49] Trueman.

this dinner party's position on absolute truth?' No, you don't, because it's a non-sensical question. [50]

Jones' statement is quite helpful in identifying the Emergent attitude towards the church; he compares the church to a social gathering, and consequently argues that conversations surrounding truth have no relevance to social gatherings. Of course, once you remove the foundation of truth from the church, a social gathering is indeed all you are left with. However, the true church of Jesus Christ is not a social gathering, it is: 'The church of the living God, the pillar and ground of the truth. (1Tim3:15 – KJV)

A further characteristic of Emergents is not just the rejection of strong doctrinal commitments, but also a resistance to being identified as 'relativistic' or 'anti-doctrinal'. Emergents are masters of aversion, but this is also symptomatic of a non-creedal approach to ministry. In other words there is a lack of accountability, and at times even honesty, among many who on the one hand undermine the historic Christian faith but at the same time want to be considered faithful disciples of Jesus. This aversion to being identified with certain categories is clearly demonstrated by Jones during his presentation at the youth workers' convention: "I just want to know why is pinning me down so important? Why do you have such a passion to categorize me?"[51] Jones seems to be unaware that an essential mark of being a servant of God is faithfulness to the apostolic tradition:

---

[50] Tony Jones, National Youth Workers Convention, *Theoblogy*, http://theoblogy.blogspot.com/2005/11/national-youth-workers-convention.html (accessed 1[oth] October 2013).

[51] Jones.

'Follow the pattern of the sound words that you have heard from me, in the faith and love that are in Christ Jesus. (2 Tim 1:13) When leaders like Jones contradict the apostolic teaching by claiming that absolute truth is 'non-sensical', they should not be surprised when people call it for what it is, relativism. In fact, the wider church has a responsibility to call such people to account, especially when these statements are being made not only by Christians or leaders, but by leaders of leaders.

Emergent philosophy is not only unbiblical in nature, but it is also contradictory. On the one hand, it rejects absolute truth claims, but in so doing is making an absolute truth claim. It rejects propositional truth statements by making a propositional truth statement (absolute truth is 'non-sensical') and it rejects creeds but in actual fact it operates within a creedal framework. The only difference is that traditional creeds are clearly presented and therefore leaders can be held accountable, whereas the Emergent creed is often unspoken, hidden in a cloud of ambiguity, and its adherents are unaccountable to the wider church. Trueman clearly exposes this contradiction:

> I do want to make the point here that Christians are not divided between those who have creeds and confessions and those who do not; rather, they are divided between those who have public creeds and confessions that are written down and exist as public documents, subject to public scrutiny, evaluation, and critique, and those who have private creeds and confessions that are often improvised, unwritten, and thus not open to public scrutiny, not susceptible to evaluation and, crucially and ironically, not,

therefore, subject to testing by Scripture to see whether they are true.[52]

Trueman's analysis is completely applicable to Emergent philosophy. However, the Emergents are far more ambiguous than the average evangelical church which just happens to neglect the role of biblical creeds. When individual Emergents do make 'confessions' that clearly contradict the scriptures, and are questioned by the wider church, they become as slippery as an eel and refuse to be held accountable. This is not only immature, it is dishonest.

From these examples it should be clear that Emergent philosophy is contradictory, unaccountable and severed from the historic faith of the church. Christian youth work is clearly caught in the web of Emergent philosophy and has exchanged the confessions of the church for creeds of confusion and compromise.

The renowned Church of Scotland minister Rev Willie Still perceived the impact of doctrinal confusion upon the church in his time. He ushered a rallying call to the ministers of the Church of Scotland, and other churches in his day; his exhortation is relevant for Christian youth workers today:

The trouble too often with the Christian church has been that it has 'interpreted' the Bible, instead of letting it speak for itself. We know that there are wide fields for interpretation in the Scriptures (prophecy, for instance) but even there, as in all other fundamental matters, the necessary facts stand out clear and plain for all with unjaundiced eyes to see.

---

[52] Trueman.

Do we really believe the Bible sufficiently to let it speak for itself?[53]

The answer to Still's question from the ranks of Emergents and Christian youth workers is a resounding 'No!' The relativistic philosophy at the heart of Christian youth work denies the very claim that the Bible can be understood. At the heart of this worldview is a belief that language is an insufficient means of communicating and understanding truth. This suspicion of language as means of conveying truth is clearly seen in the teaching ministry of Rob Bell: "'The moment God is figured out with nice neat lines and definitions; we are no longer dealing with God."[54] Bell argues further:

> The Christian faith is mysterious to the core. It is about things and beings that ultimately can't be put into words. Language fails. And if we do definitively put God into words, we have at that very moment made God something God is not.[55]

Such a statement is a complete contradiction of the Christian faith; a denial of the scriptures which God has given as a 'revelation' of himself; and rejection of the sufficiency of the doctrinal formulations and confessions of the historic Christian church. Welcome to the indefinable God of Emergent philosophy and Christian youth work, a God, who, like play dough, can be squeezed into any shape and size. Of course we, as humans, can

---

[53] William Still, *The Letters of William Still*, (Edinburgh: Banner of Truth Trust, 1984), 46-47.
[54] Rob Bell Velvet Elvis: Repainting the Christian Faith, (New York: Harper Collins, 2005), 25.
[55] Bell, 32.

never exhaust the knowledge of God; our knowledge of God is not even comparable to a drop of rain in the Atlantic ocean; but this does not mean we cannot understand the very things he has revealed about himself to us through the scriptures. Trueman highlights how this approach to language and truth actively conflicts with Christian expressions of truth: 'Any force that undermines general confidence in language as a medium capable of conveying information or of constituting relationships is also a force that strikes at the validity of creeds and confessions.' The consequence of this philosophy is that youth leaders are sinking in sands of uncertainty as they try to reach young people with the Christian faith. This approach is counter-productive and disconnected, not only from historic evangelicalism, but also the historic Christian faith.

Willie Still tackles the theological culture of confusion and compromise head on:

> If the present climate of theological opinion and biblical scholarship is to prevail, we fear that it is going to take many so long to determine what they do believe and what they do not, that this generation may have passed into the Hell about which the modern church is so uncertain, before they can make up their minds. It is the problem of this, the problem of that – all problems, no solutions; all fog and darkness, no light! And, in any case, where is the apostolic conviction to come from in a Gospel of shreds and patches? It is the surrender of the will to intellectual conviction of the Truth which alone inflames men's hearts and sets them on fire for God. The Gospel will never again run through Scotland and 'set the heather on fire' until the men of the Church of Scotland sacrifice their pride of intellect and fall humbly before Him whose Word is too great for us to

ever fully understand, and then rise to proclaim simply like faithful errand boys. Heralds do not need great intellects (indeed too much may mar their service!). The defence of God's Word is with God He will look after that! The proclamation of it is with us, and woe betide us if we fail! For if we do, God will find himself a living Church elsewhere, and by it He will work, and will by-pass us to our everlasting shame! 'All scripture is God breathed' says Paul to Timothy, 'and is profitable.' No Christian needs more than this to make him an authoritative herald of God's word. . . May God grant us all to be so convinced, cleansed and inspired by His Word ourselves, that we proclaim it with convicting and converting power, to his glory, not ours.[56]

Willie Still's rallying call is not just a needed corrective for the Church of Scotland, it is a corrective for the church *in* Scotland. It is a corrective for modern evangelicalism and the Christian youth work and youth ministry it has spawned. Willie Still's urgent appeal is much closer to the mind and spirit of historical evangelicalism than the current diluted and polluted version we see today.

The key purpose of this book is to highlight the need for gospel-centred youth work and ministry. If youth work and ministry is to become gospel-centred, then there needs to be a reconnection between Christian youth work and ministry and the Word of God and the creeds of the Christian church. Christian youth workers and ministries need to develop a confessional approach to Christian youth work and ministry.

---

[56] Still, 47-48.

5 The Making of a Missionary

What does it take to be a youth worker? What qualifications are needed? What skills are required to work with young people? What are the desired characteristics of a Christian youth worker? I have observed these questions being discussed in various youth work training sessions, whether the discussion was taking place among professional practitioners or volunteers: the list of answers is both endless and diverse and reflective of the varying understandings relating to the purpose of Christian youth work. However, one way to measure what churches and youth organisations consider to be the essential characteristics of Christian youth workers, is to examine adverts for youth work vacancies. Adverts have limited space and therefore tend to get straight to the point. They focus on the job that needs to be done, the essential skills and the desired characteristics of the potential candidate. The following vacancy adverts are worth thinking about:[57]

Example One

We are looking for someone who is approachable, fun and who can relate well to young people. You will be joining a team of some of the nicest people we've ever met, in a great project that helps young people grow, belong and get to know Jesus. You should know how to

---

[57] Specific details of organisations have been omitted.

have a laugh, and be prepared to get involved in some crazy activities.

Drawing on your experience, and with our team of staff and volunteers, you will help young people develop resilience, community capacity and leadership skills, and respond to the good news about Jesus.

Example Two

This is an opportunity to work with a wide range of young people of secondary school age expending on the work of the Association; creating a space for young people to relax, talk to youth workers and take part in social activities and programmes. To encourage young people to reach their potential and the opportunity to explore the Christian faith.

The successful applicant will be a leader, a team builder, an encourager, an excellent communicator, have proven skills in networking, be able to demonstrate previous success in community/church work or a similar role, be approachable and sensitive, respect confidentiality, have a good sense of humour and an active personal Christian faith.

Example Three

We are now seeking:

A committed and practising Christian willing to join the team and the church

A highly motivated and experienced individual with excellent interpersonal, youth work and management skills/qualifications, including the ability to manage budgets and to secure potential future funding for the role and the project as a whole

A dynamic and creative leader of programme, volunteer and centre management, as well as community engagement.

Someone able to assist in establishing this exciting new youth project and develop its relationship with the church.

Example Four

We are looking to employ a youth worker, the new staff member will need to be:
a) A committed Christian.
b) A qualified youth worker: JNC, Degree, other equivalent or relevant experience.
c) Creative and experienced in developing church and community based youth programmes.
d) Passionate about youth discipleship & seeing young people grow and develop.
e) IT literate, good at planning and organising.

Example Five

We are recruiting a development worker who meets the following person specification.

Experience and understanding of schools work, including a working knowledge of schools work practices such as safeguarding, data protection, and health and safety regulations

A good ability to develop, plan and work in a team, as well as experience of project management and leading a team

Christian Commitment: active involvement in a local church, and participation in the wider Christian community

Because this post requires the post-holder to be able to articulate and demonstrate the Christian faith, it is therefore a Genuine Occupational Requirement of the post that the person appointed should be an actively practicing Christian, demonstrated through personal belief, full participation in the life of a local church, and through lifestyle.

The above examples are very insightful in highlighting what churches and youth organisations consider to be the most important characteristics of a Christian youth worker. While each example has its own distinctive style, on the whole, the emphasis is on *professional* skills, qualifications and experience. While all of the examples mention that being a Christian is an essential requirement, in three out of the four examples, more time is spent on the details of professional characteristics than is spent on the details of spiritual characteristics. Example five is an exception to this pattern and moves beyond vague expressions such as 'practicing Christian' or 'Committed Christian' and lists specific requirements such as personal faith, active involvement in a church and a lifestyle which reflects their faith.

What these vacancy adverts demonstrate is that 'Christian' youth work, which predates professional youth work, is attempting to establish itself as a profession. To what extent the adjective 'Christian' in Christian youth work plays in defining Christian youth work is not always clear. In other words, the pursuit of professional skills and competences has created a situation where youth work is defined more by professional values than it is by the Christian faith. Instead of professional skills *serving* the mission of the church, professional values and practices now *define* the mission of the church. Consequently, the qualifications for youth workers and characteristics expected from them are more defined by professionalism than they are the Bible. John Piper highlights the negative consequences of professionalism within the context of pastoral ministry in his book *Brothers We Are Not Professionals*; the issues raised by Piper relating to pastoral ministry are equally relevant for Christian youth work:

> Is there professional praying? Professional trusting in God's promises? Professional weeping over souls? Professional musing on the depths of revelation? Professional rejoicing in the truth? Professional praising God's name? Professional treasuring the riches of Christ? Professional walking by the Spirit? Professional exercise of spiritual gifts? Professional dealing with demons? Professional pleading with backsliders? Professional perseverance in a hard marriage? Professional playing with children? Professional courage in the face of persecution? Professional patience with everyone?[58]

Piper goes on to explain the point he is seeking to drive home:

> These are not marginal activities in the pastoral life. They are central. They are the essence. Why do we choke on the word professional in those connections? Because professionalization carries the connotation of an education, a set of skills, and a set of guild-defined standards which are possible without faith in Jesus. Professionalism is not supernatural. The heart of ministry is. [59]

This is exactly what has happened in Christian youth work contexts; however, the fact that professionalism can be carried out without faith in Christ is not the only problem, an even deeper problem is the fact that professional values actually conflict with and undermine the mission of the

---

[58] John Piper, *Brothers We Are Not Professionals*, (Nashville Tennessee: B&H Publishing, 2013), Kindle.

[59] Piper.

church. Piper demonstrates this principle within the context of pastoral ministry:

> Ministry is professional in those areas of competency where the life of faith and the life of unbelief overlap. Which means two things. First, that overlapping area can never be central. Therefore, professionalism should always be marginal, not central; optional, not crucial. And second, the pursuit of professionalism will push the supernatural center more and more into the corner while ministry becomes a set of secular competencies with a religious veneer.[60]

In other words, while there are certain areas where the secular and the sacred overlap, for youth work this would include areas such as child protection policies, and risk assessments, however professionalism should never be given the defining role in ministry contexts. Piper highlights the consequences of professionalism being given central place; he argues that spirituality will be forced out by secularism and our ministries will masquerade as Christian service when in fact the Christian youth worker is simply performing a 'set of secular competencies with a religious veneer.' The centrality of professionalism is the reason why so many Christian youth work job advertisements focus more on secular skills than they do on spiritual characteristics. The centrality of professionalism is also the reason why Christian youth work projects will often devote their energies on secular objectives rather than spiritual objectives.

Piper further argues that professionalism is damaging the unique calling of many pastors:

---

[60] Piper.

We pastors are being killed by the professionalizing of the pastoral ministry. The mentality of the professional is not the mentality of the prophet. It is not the mentality of the slave of Christ. Professionalism has nothing to do with the essence and heart of the Christian ministry. The more professional we long to be, the more spiritual death we will leave in our wake. For there is no professional childlikeness (Matt. 18:3); there is no professional tender-heartedness (Eph. 4:32); there is no professional panting after God (Ps. 42:1).[61]

Professionalism does not only kill pastors, it kills the calling of many youth workers. A common pattern I recognised among many youth work students is the deadening effect that Christian youth work studies had upon their missional fervour. Students would begin college on fire for God but slowly and surely the fire would be extinguished by the waters of professionalism. Before long, evangelism was no longer important, Bible teaching was not important, and essential factors such as preaching and church commitment were considered hindrances to youth work.

Piper highlights the key reason why professionalism kills Christian ministry; he demonstrates that Christianity and secular professions have different aims and goals:

You cannot professionalize the love for His appearing without killing it. And it is being killed. The aims of our ministry are eternal and spiritual. They are not shared by any of the professions. It is precisely by the failure to see this that we are dying . . . We are most emphatically not part of a social team sharing goals with other professionals. Our goals are an offense; they are foolishness (1 Cor. 1:23). The

---

[61] Piper.

professionalization of the ministry is a constant threat to the offense of the gospel. It is a threat to the profoundly spiritual nature of our work. I have seen it often: the love of professionalism (parity among the world's professionals) kills a man's belief that he is sent by God to save people from hell and to make them Christ-exalting, spiritual aliens in the world.[62]

When professionalism is given a central place within Christian service, it has a devastating effect on the mission of the church.[63] Consequently, those who sense a calling to work with young people find themselves pursuing objectives, training and methods which conflict with the heart of mission.

If professionalism focuses on characteristics which conflict with Christian ministry, what are the characteristics that should mark Christian youth work and ministry? What are the biblical qualifications for those who would seek to serve young people? What characteristics should mark those who want to lead young people? One of the challenges we encounter in answering these questions is the fact that the Bible does not include 'youth workers' or 'youth leaders' in its list of gifts, ministries or offices.

The world of young people, the world of the adolescent, and the world of the 'teenager', is in many ways a social construction which emerged in 20th century western society. The emergence of youth cultures is largely economically driven; on the one hand, it has led to the division of young people and adults, but on the other hand, it has also led to the dominance of youth culture across the generations. It was not so long ago that grandparents, parents and teenagers were

---

[62] Piper.

[63] Appendix

characterised by different fashion styles, music tastes and social activities. This has changed dramatically due to the dominance of youth culture; this can be seen by the fact that many grannies (and in some instances great-grannies) have traded blue rinse for tattoos, Patsy Cline for Pink, and Bingo for Facebook.

However, while many of the challenges surrounding the emergence of the 'teenage' phenomenon are the consequence of social engineering, young people are nevertheless part of the wider community. The church is called to serve the community and reach out with the gospel; therefore, this work should not exclude specific work with young people. Some pastors of traditional denominations perceive youth work as completely divisive (and at times it has been) but this does not mean that serving young people must lead to division any more than pastoral work among the elderly leads to division.

From this point of view, our approaches to working with young people need to be drawn from the wider scriptural guidance on mission, service and leadership. In other words, the characteristics of youth workers must reflect the characteristics which the Bible teaches should be demonstrated among those who are sent as messengers of gospel, leaders of local churches and servants of mercy and compassion. Since Christian youth work and ministry tends to be a combination of mission work, leadership and practical service, we can learn the required qualifications and characteristics by looking at the biblical qualifications and characteristics of missionaries, elders and deacons.

Before we look at biblical ministries and the qualifications of such ministries, we also need to explore some of the characteristics of youth ministry. Youth ministry has also flirted with professionalism in its own way, only the professionalism of youth ministry is not the values and skills of the more established professions, it is the professionalism of the entertainment industry. Consequently many leaders in youth ministry contexts have created an identity which is a fusion of the celebrity and the rock star. Youth leaders in this context follow the elaborate fashions of celebrities and in some cases have taken on pseudonyms in the style of contemporary music artists. In this context, image is everything. Consequently, the dominating role that entertainment and image play within youth ministry contexts also pushes out the more essential characteristics of Christian ministry that we are about to explore.

Mission

It is interesting to note that some secular informal educators have emphasised a vocational element which underpins their community and youth work: 'For many, informal education is more than a job, it is a calling.'[64] If this is true for secular youth workers, it should be even more so for Christian youth workers. If, as we have already explored, the pursuit of professionalism has a tendency to kill the missional motivation of Christian youth work, the first step to restoring the missional purpose must be to rediscover the source of the mission: the call of God. The word *Mission* is from the Latin *missio* which means "sending."[65]

---

[64] Tony Jeffs, Mark K Smith *Informal Education* (Derbyshire, Education Now Publishing, 1999), 7.
[65] Packer, (1993), 223-224.

The church bases its own missional purpose in the original sending of the apostles (sent ones):

> And Jesus came and said to them, "All authority in heaven and on earth has been given to me. Go therefore and make disciples of all nations, baptizing them in the name of the Father and of the Son and of the Holy Spirit, teaching them to observe all that I have commanded you. And behold, I am with you always, to the end of the age." (Matt 28:18-20)

If Christian youth work or youth ministry is not deeply rooted in this calling, it is hard to see in what sense it can actually be considered Christian or ministry. Of course, many of the professionalised youth work projects and youth ministries do believe that they are rooted in the missional call. Many youth workers see the professional values, principles and methods as an effective means of being equipped for mission. Yet in all the pursuit of professionalism the most basic means of empowering and the essential qualification for ministry that Jesus spoke to his disciples about is often overlooked:

> Then he said to them, "These are my words that I spoke to you while I was still with you, that everything written about me in the Law of Moses and the Prophets and the Psalms must be fulfilled." Then he opened their minds to understand the Scriptures, and said to them, "Thus it is written, that the Christ should suffer and on the third day rise from the dead, and that repentance and forgiveness of sins should be proclaimed in his name to all nations, beginning from Jerusalem. You are witnesses of these things. And behold, I am sending the promise of my Father upon you. But stay in the city until you are clothed with power from on high." (Luke 24:44-49)

A number of things happen to the disciples in this text, and they must happen to us too, if we are to be of any use to God. Firstly, they were instructed in the word of God: 'These are my words that I spoke to you while I was still with you, that everything written about me in the Law of Moses and the Prophets and the Psalms must be fulfilled.' Not only were they taught the scriptures, they are shown how the scriptures point to Jesus.' During my time as a youth work student we were studying hermeneutics (principles of biblical interpretation). We looked at feminist hermeneutics, African hermeneutics and Latin-American hermeneutics (all of which focused on an interpretation of scripture as through the eyes of marginalised people groups). It was suggested that we consider the possibility of youth hermeneutics (a distinct framework of interpretation that young people can adopt). In another project, a method of Bible study was developed which enabled young people to arrive at their own interpretations; in other words, there was to be no formal teaching at all. The community of young people would decide what the text meant.

Now, I understand what these two approaches are trying to achieve. Those who employ these methods are trying to demonstrate a way of interpreting scripture which values the creativity and contribution of young people. They are attempting to integrate Bible study in a way that values the educational principles of empowerment which are enshrined by informal education. But here is a novel idea, how about a way of interpreting scriptures which demonstrates that we value Jesus? After all, the Bible is all about him: 'Everything written about me in the Law of Moses and the Prophets and the Psalms must be fulfilled.'

Not only were the disciples instructed in the scriptures, the Bible tells us that: 'He (Jesus) opened their minds to understand the Scriptures.' In other words, they did not just have information but they also had illumination. This is what the Holy Spirit does for us; he takes the text and opens up the eyes of our heart. This too is one of the greatest needs of the hour, a fresh glimpse of God as revealed in the Word of God and brought home to our hearts by the Spirit of God.

Not only were they taught and spiritually enlightened, they were commissioned as witnesses. 'Witnessing' was a phrase I used to hear a lot when I first became a Christian; however, it seems to be out of vogue these days. Nevertheless, the church is still called to be a witness. I remember a youth worker reacting negatively to a question which I had addressed to another youth worker who was working for the same organisation as me; I asked: 'Do you have many opportunities to share the gospel?' Before the person I addressed the question to could answer, the other youth worker exploded: 'Why do you assume that you need to speak to them about God? God might be working in their life anyway!' Yet surely if God is working in the life of a young person this would be all the more reason to speak to them about Christ? In fact, this would be the best time to speak to them since the Holy Spirit is preparing the heart. As uncomfortable as it is for Christians living in a post-modern context, the church is called to be a witness of Jesus Christ.

Yet even having been taught the scriptures, experienced illumination, and commissioned as witnesses, the disciples were still not equipped. Jesus told them that they still lacked what they needed to get the job done: "I am sending the promise of my Father upon you. But stay in the city until you are clothed with power from on high." The empowering of the Holy Spirit is the primary means by which the church engages in effective mission. Charles Spurgeon knew how essential the empowering of the Spirit was:

> The Saviour said to the eleven that they were to wait at Jerusalem till they had received power by the Holy Ghost coming upon them. This is what we want; we want the Holy Ghost. We often speak about this; but, in truth, it is unspeakable, the power of the Holy Ghost, mysterious, divine. When it comes upon a man, he is bathed in the very essence of the Deity. The atmosphere about him becomes the life and power of God.
>
> Now, beloved, I have not time fully to describe this endowment; I have only mentioned one or two points in which it is seen, but this endowment is what we need before we can do anything for Christ. Do you always think enough of this? The teacher prepares her lesson; but does she also prepare herself by seeking the power of the Holy Spirit? The minister studies his text; but does he ask for a baptism of the Holy Ghost? I am afraid that this spiritual qualification, the most essential of all, is frequently overlooked. Then, the Lord have mercy upon us! The soldier had better go to battle without sword or rifle, the artilleryman had better wheel up his gun without powder or shot, than that we should attempt to win a soul until first of all the Holy Spirit has given us power. Power must go with the word that is preached or taught if any large result is to follow; and that power must first be in the man who speaks that word.[66]

---

[66] Charles Spurgeon, "Witnessing Better than Knowing the Future", A Sermon (No. 2330) Intended for Reading on Lord's-Day, October 15th, 1893, Metropolitan Tabernacle, Newington On Thursday Evening, August 29th, 1889.

In my own work with young people over a ten year period, I can honestly say that the most effective presentations of the gospel were the messages that were marked by the empowering of the Spirit. Very often, these messages were the most simple and straightforward, and they were also the messages that were birthed out of deep prayer and intercession. One of these instances in particular was during a youth residential; I was working alongside a team of student youth workers. We decided as a team that we would include an extra element into the week's programme. Each evening we decided to include hot chocolate and muffins, a time of praise and some short gospel or testimony presentations. One afternoon, after the morning sessions, I was reading my Bible devotional for that day. The topic happened to be about hell. As I read the text and the accompanying notes, I sensed the Lord convict me deeply. I realised that we had been doing a great job of teaching the young people that a relationship with Jesus was a good way of life, but we had not told them that a relationship with Jesus was the only way to be saved. I got on my knees and I cried out to God, saying, 'Lord if you want me to share this message, you must give me the compassion and the spiritual authority that is needed.' In other words, people needed to know that these were not just my words, but they were the very words of the living God. I chose for my text John 3:16 and the message was very simple: if those who do believe '*shall not* perish', those who do not believe *shall* perish.' The word came in gentleness but with power. One young guy in particular came

---

http://www.spurgeon.org/sermons/2330.htm (accessed 13th March 2014).

under a cloud of conviction for the next few days. On the final night he placed his trust in Christ and his countenance was transformed. In his own words he said 'Everything is so clear.'

I simply share this to demonstrate that my own experience has confirmed the teaching of scriptures and the testimony of God's servants throughout church history; when all is said and done, it is the Holy Spirit who does the work.

Deacons

Generally speaking, the Protestant church has recognised two offices: elders and deacons.[67] 'Deacon' is taken from the Greek word for servant. We first encounter deacons in Acts Chapter 6 when a need emerges for people to be involved in distributing food to the poor. While the role of the deacons in Acts 6 was of a compassionate and practical nature, the qualification for fulfilling the role is very insightful. The apostles instructed the church to: 'Pick out from among you seven men of good repute, full of the Spirit and of wisdom.' (Acts 6:3) What is particularly interesting is that although the task was practical, the qualifications needed were spiritual. The potential candidate was to have a good reputation, fruit of the Spirit, and was to be known for having wisdom. This is a sharp contrast to most of the person specifications we looked at earlier. The modern church looks for secular skills whereas the early church looked for spirituality.

Later, the apostle Paul would write to Timothy and give him instructions in regards to how the church should be governed. Among these

---

[67] Anglicans recognise Bishops as a third office.

instructions are further qualifications for those who fulfil the role of deacons:

> Deacons likewise must be dignified, not double-tongued, not addicted to much wine, not greedy for dishonest gain. They must hold the mystery of the faith with a clear conscience. And let them also be tested first; then let them serve as deacons if they prove themselves blameless. Their wives likewise must be dignified, not slanderers, but sober-minded, faithful in all things. Let deacons each be the husband of one wife, managing their children and their own households well. For those who serve well as deacons gain a good standing for themselves and also great confidence in the faith that is in Christ Jesus. (1Tim 3: 8-12)

Again we see the contrast between the emphasis of the modern church with the emphasis of the early church. The early church considered Christ-like character, holiness and a good reputation to be the essential characteristic for serving the church. It is important to stress that the primary role of the deacons was not to teach, or even evangelise, these were the folks who were engaging in mercy ministries.

Elders (Pastors and teachers)

The following scriptures identify the characteristics of church leaders. We mentioned earlier, that 'youth worker' or 'youth pastor' is not an office, but since the role of many church youth workers, or even youth 'pastors', involves leading and teaching young people, the required qualifications for eldership are well worth considering.

The saying is trustworthy: If anyone aspires to the office of overseer, he desires a noble task. Therefore an overseer must be above reproach, the husband of one wife, sober-minded, self-controlled, respectable, hospitable, able to teach, not a drunkard, not violent but gentle, not quarrelsome, not a lover of money. He must manage his own household well, with all dignity keeping his children submissive, for if someone does not know how to manage his own household, how will he care for God's church? He must not be a recent convert, or he may become puffed up with conceit and fall into the condemnation of the devil. Moreover, he must be well thought of by outsiders, so that he may not fall into disgrace, into a snare of the devil. (I Tim 3:1-7)

This is why I left you in Crete, so that you might put what remained into order, and appoint elders in every town as I directed you— if anyone is above reproach, the husband of one wife, and his children are believers and not open to the charge of debauchery or insubordination. For an overseer, as God's steward, must be above reproach. He must not be arrogant or quick-tempered or a drunkard or violent or greedy for gain, but hospitable, a lover of good, self-controlled, upright, holy, and disciplined. He must hold firm to the trustworthy word as taught, so that he may be able to give instruction in sound doctrine and also to rebuke those who contradict it. (Titus 1:5-9)

Character and creed

The emphasis in both of these texts can be summed up in two words: character and creed. A godly lifestyle; a hospitable heart; sound doctrine; and the ability to teach; are essential requirements for church ministry roles that place a person in a leadership and teaching capacity. Exploring these characteristics could open up other areas of discussion such as: how are youth pastors different to pastors? Should youth pastors be elders? If Paul warns against putting recent converts into eldership, is there an equal danger in putting recent converts into youth leadership? If new believers are placed in leadership, what safeguards or accountability structures are being put in place to help them deal with pride? These are all important questions, which we don't have time to explore here, but they are worth considering.

I'm deeply aware that drawing the leadership criteria for Christian youth work and youth ministry from the biblical qualifications for Church leadership is in many ways to remove some of the glitz and glamour which often surrounds youth work and ministry. It rescues Christian work with young people from the domain of the superstar celebrity or sophisticated professional and grounds it in a foundation of ordinariness. But it is this ordinariness which may well bring back the supernatural power of God into our work with young people. After all, the treasure of God is deposited in jars of clay. (2 Cor 4:7)

6 Gospel-Centred Youth Work and Ministry

Having considered many of the factors which compete with a gospel-centred approach to Christian youth work and ministry, the following principles can be of help in grounding our youth work and ministry in a more mission focused approach. However, in raising the following suggestions, it is important to emphasise that I *am not* claiming to have a pre-packaged version of Christian youth work and ministry (we have enough of those); I *am* instead calling for a gospel-centred vision.

An unrestricted gospel

In order to be truly missional there must be unrestricted gospel motivation, intention and communication. In other words, the gospel must not be chained because we have submitted to the secular values of pluralism, relativism, and inclusivism. If we pursue funding that causes us to submit to secular objectives which cause the gospel to no longer be the primary motivation, and to no longer be communicated freely, we have redefined our goals and agenda. We are no longer missional. The gospel should be the heartbeat of all that we do, and we should always be free to communicate the gospel. If youth work and ministry is to remain (or become) gospel-centred, the gospel must define the central purpose. To remain gospel-centred in our ministries is a constant battle with the world, the flesh and the devil. There are always competing priorities, in the current context of youth work and ministry, obsession with relevance has led to the embracing of the values of the secular professions or the entertainment industry. The pursuit of relevance itself has become one of the major contributors to a non-gospel-centred approach. Peter Kreeft insightfully declares: "When relevance becomes a god, the relevant thing to do is to smash the idol."

Responsive to needs

Missional youth work and ministry should not lead to an insular approach. All around us are people who are suffering. Sometimes we can shield ourselves from this suffering; the more affluent we are, the more we are able to distance ourselves from the more unpleasant aspects of society. Like the rich man, we live in luxury, blind to the suffering that lies on our very doorstep. Many young people live in a world of unemployment, social turmoil, substance abuse and at-risk behaviour; that world is real and is not far from the places where many of us gather on a weekly basis to worship God. Jesus said: 'The harvest is plentiful, but the labourers are few.' The tragic irony is that many churches are dying in the middle of a harvest field.

For many years I was involved in 'detached youth work'; this is a model of youth work which seeks to identify where young people are hanging out; what provision exists for them; what gaps there are in the provision; and then explores ways in which unmet needs can be met. Detached work involves communication with the young people and other agencies. In theory, detached youth work has been distinct from outreach work. Outreach work usually involves going out with a set agenda, such as inviting young people to an event or youth club or even street evangelism, Detached work does not so much set out with an invitation to an existing service, but goes out to find out what the young people need and then works towards meeting that need. Strictly speaking, detached work in its purest form would exclude evangelism. In my own youth work career I was involved in recruiting, training and coordinating teams of detached youth workers. Sadly the project was bound up in secular funding objectives which excluded the promotion of the gospel. However, I do believe that the detached approach can be adopted and adapted so that it *serves* the purpose of mission instead of *redefining* it. Of course, when we do this, it will no longer be detached youth work in the strictest sense – but our ultimate aim is to be faithful to Christ's mission, not secular informal educational principles. At a very basic level, detached work is simply identifying the needs of our community and then responding to those needs; this could be utilised to fulfil the churches' call to be 'salt and light.'

Integrated with the local church

One of the essential ways in which youth work and youth ministry can maintain a missional approach to Christian youth work is to work hard to ensure that the work is integrated with the life of the local church. Looking back at the height of my own youth work career, I recognise that this was one of the weakest areas. I was working with a para-church organisation; we were working with some of the most 'hard-to-reach' young people and almost every waking hour was spent at the youth project. In many ways, para-church became a substitute for church, and I know that this has been the experience of many other youth workers, but somehow it seemed justifiable since we felt that we were reaching young people when the churches were not. This was a mistake.

Another difficulty with this particular parachurch was the fact that it had also lost its strong connection with local churches. At one time the churches were the driving force of this organisation; however, as the organisation began to pursue secular funding, goals and objectives, the link with the churches became weaker and weaker until the link was ultimately severed. When this happens to an organisation, the primary purpose has been lost. Instead of existing to further the purpose of the gospel, the organisation is instead driven by a need to survive. In order to keep the machine running, the organisation will chase after every pot of funding in order to keep itself alive. When this happens, the aims of the organisation are no longer shaped by mission, but by the objectives of whatever funder happens to have money.

Not only must our work be integrated into the life of the local church, but our message and methods must be integrated with the historic creeds of the church. Gary Gilley, in his insightful book *This Little Church Went to Market: Is the Modern Church Reaching Out or Selling Out?*, argues that the modern evangelical church has replaced the Word of God with psychology; worship with entertainment; and evangelism with market driven techniques. The issues that have been identified in youth work and youth ministry contexts are a direct consequence of the current state of evangelicalism. In order to correct this, Christian youth work and ministry needs to rediscover the core doctrines that once marked evangelicalism. There needs to be a return to: the sovereignty of God; the divine inspiration, authority and sufficiency of scripture; the doctrine of sin; substitutionary atonement; justification by faith alone; regeneration by the Holy Spirit; the doctrine of the church and preaching on the second appearing of the Lord Jesus Christ.

Getting the balance right

Christianity is full of tensions; if we don't strike the balance, we tend to fall into error. This is true in the spheres of doctrine, mission, and our work with young people. Many of the errors we have identified in the previous chapters have emerged because we have not got the balance right. For example, the over-emphasis on God's love in youth ministry messages is a consequence of not having a fuller understanding of God which would also include his holiness, justice, wisdom and sovereignty. In the realm of mission, the tension between social action and evangelism has been exacerbated due to humanistic cultural pressures. Christian youth work and youth ministry has also struggled to maintain a balance between the competing objectives of entertainment and contemplation; social activities and spiritual activities; and exploration of the gospel and declaration of the gospel. An inability to navigate these tensions wisely has led to many of the imbalances which we have explored in this book. Entertainment, space for socialising, dialogue, social action all play an important part in our work with young people, but when these things define the purpose and methods of youth work and ministry, we have already lost the centrality of the gospel. When entertainment dominates, there is no room for contemplation; when socialising takes priority, the spiritual is side-lined; and when social justice eclipses evangelism, all we have is humanism.

What will it take to reach young people with the gospel? What does gospel-centred youth work and ministry look like in practice? Kevin DeYoung argues that it is both easier and harder than we think:

> Reaching the next generation—whether they are outside the church or sitting there bored in your church—is easier and harder than you think. It's easier because you don't have to get a degree in postmodern literary theory or go to a bunch of stupid movies. You don't have to say "sweet" or "bling" or know what LOL or IMHO means. You don't have to listen to . . . well, whatever people listen to these days. You don't have to be on Twitter, watch The Office, or imbibe fancy coffees. You just have to be like Jesus. That's it. So the easy part is you don't have to be with it. The hard part is you have to be with him. If you walk with God and walk with people, you'll reach the next generation.[68]

In other words, drawing young people to Jesus is primarily a matter of walking with God and walking with them. Paul demonstrated this in his letter to the Thessalonians: 'So, being affectionately desirous of you, we were ready to share with you not only the gospel of God but also our own selves, because you had become very dear to us.' (Thess 2:8)

The principles laid out by Paul and DeYoung may not seem very glamorous, but they are time

---

[68] Kevin DeYoung *Don't Call it a Comeback*: *The Old Faith for a New Day*, (Wheaton IL: Crossway, 2011). Kindle

tested and true. In my own youth work practice, I can honestly say that one of the best seasons was before I went to study theology and youth work. I coordinated youth work at a youth centre at the heart of a large town on the outskirts of Glasgow. Many of the young people would be considered by professionals as 'hard-to-reach'. The work flourished, grew, and many young people transitioned from being hostile towards Christianity to being very open. Initially we opened at set times; eventually the youth office became a twelve hours a day, six days a week drop-in centre. Young people dropped by on a daily basis looking for support, or just space away from family conflict or at times seeking spiritual guidance. The whole thing was a shambles, professionally speaking, but it was relationally and spiritually alive. There was a genuine heart for the young people among the team, Jesus was very real to those who were working with the young people, and that started to rub off.

In many ways this brings me to my concluding thought. This book has focused on the two predominant models of Christian work with young people. It has focused on the professional youth worker and the contemporary youth pastor. Both of these models need to undergo a major reformation if they are to become gospel-centred.

However, there is another 'model' which I have not mentioned. Perhaps it is an even more common model than the other two. It is the model of youth work and ministry that is led by an army of unsung heroes. It is led by individuals, married couples and countless teams of volunteers who give up their time; open their homes; turn up every week to a church youth club; and who are available as a listening ear for the young people who attend their church (be they many or few). They are non-specialists; they perhaps lack professional skills; they are not on the church pay roll and they probably don't feel they are doing anything of great significance. Yet the reality is these people are living out the gospel-centred approach. They perhaps do 'relational evangelism' better than the 'full-time worker', because the relationship is not based on a professional and client model or a celebrity and fan model; their 'relational evangelism' is rooted in the family of God model. While the Christian youth work theorists are busy developing theories and principles and while the innovators are busting their gut trying to develop the next new thing; an army of nameless and faceless church members are simply caring for young people, journeying with them and magnifying the gospel of Christ in word and deed.

Appendix: What's the Point?

What is the aim of Christian youth work? If you ask any group of Christians who work with young people this question, you are guaranteed to get a variety of answers. The responses are endless: 'spread the gospel', 'make disciples', 'enable young people to reach their full potential', 'social, emotional, physical and spiritual development', and the one that causes trained youth workers to have an internal explosion: 'to keep young people off the streets.' However, before we think about *how* we should approach Christian youth work and ministry, we need to think about *why* we want to develop a Christian youth work or ministry. Informal educator Carole Pughe explores and analyses the purpose of Christian youth work in her article: 'Christian Youth Work: Evangelism or Social Action?' Pughe explores both the variety of approaches to Christian Youth work and the importance of understanding the role of purpose within Christian youth work and ministry:

> Christian youth work has varying purposes, encompassing different approaches. The particular purpose a Christian worker seeks will have implications for the methods and content of their work.[69]

---

[69] Carole Pughe, "Christian Youth work: Evangelism or Social action?" Infed
http://www.infed.org.uk/christianeducation/christianyw.htm (accessed 20th Nov 2013).

In other words, the variety of approaches to Christian youth work is a result, not of multiple methods, but of the diversity of purpose. Pughe understands what many Christian youth workers and youth leaders often misunderstand: purpose shapes practice. What we do springs from what we believe. Our ideology of youth work will shape our methodology; for example: if we think the Bible is no longer relevant, this will be reflected in the absence of Bible related activities in our youth programme. If we think it is important that young people hear the good news of Jesus Christ, this too will be evident in our youth programme.

We live in an age where most things are instant, most of us live busy lives and therefore do not have much time or patience for the 'What?' and 'Why?': we just want the 'How?'. Give me 'Seven Steps to a Successful Youth Ministry' and I'm on my way. Show me a model that is drawing in large crowds of young people and I'll adopt it in my church. This is called pragmatism; pragmatism says: 'Who cares about the rights and wrongs, or the truths and errors, just give me something that works. If it works, it must be good.' Of course, such thinking is tragic, especially in the realm of Christian ministry. It is pragmatic thinking that has caused many western churches to judge the success of a ministry on the basis of its numbers, popularity and slick marketing. It is pragmatic thinking that has neglected the more essential aspects of biblical Christianity: truth, grace, and righteousness.

Two of the most common approaches to Christian youth work, certainly within evangelicalism, are Christian youth work and youth ministry. Christian youth work draws its principles and practice from secular youth work and many of its projects are financed by secular funders.

Christian youth work has developed its own profession, degree programmes and accreditation for youth workers. On the other hand, Christian youth ministry is less specialised and is usually funded by the church. Youth work tends to focus on personal and social development, whereas youth ministry tends to focus on providing alternative activities for church youth in order to keep them in church and away from the world. Youth ministry will also have more of a focus on evangelism and discipleship. Both youth ministry and Christian youth work operate within local churches or para-church organisations.

For approximately ten years, I have been involved in both Christian youth work and youth ministry, I have worked with young people in the context of the local church and para-church. In all of these settings, I have worked with teams of staff and volunteers who are passionate about making a difference in the lives of young people. I have seen the blessing of God in the various projects and I have experienced the joy of seeing young people develop and grow in each of these environments. However, in all of these contexts, I have also observed similar problems and weaknesses: either the work with young people lacks *clarity of purpose,* or its purpose is more *defined by secular culture* than it is by the Word of God.

Professional Christian youth work has adopted the purpose, principles and practices of secular youth work which derives its theory and practice from Informal Education. Informal Education and secular youth work are focused not just on the personal development of young people but also the political engagement of young people.

Informal Education

The informal education approach to youth work is based upon western social, political and educational values and principles. Informal education, in contrast to formal education, emphasises the learning that takes place outside the school classroom; in particular, the learning that takes place through relationships and 'real life' situations. Youth work is an example of informal education, since it seeks to promote the development and wellbeing of young people in situations other than the school classroom.

Informal education (the idea that people learn in informal social situations) has been around as long as people have; however, informal education as a profession is a fairly recent development and has its origins in the 20th century. Professional informal education is much more than learning that takes place in informal situations. Professional informal education is defined by a particular political, social and philosophical context. The philosophy of informal education is intrinsically linked to the values of secular humanism that have replaced Christianity as the dominant western worldview.

In order for Christian youth organisations to receive funding; for their workers to receive accreditation; and for their work to be considered credible, many Christian youth work projects have had to embody the values, theory and practice of informal education. This is why Christian youth work projects have mission statements that are identified more closely with secularism than Christianity. The secularisation of Christian youth work can clearly be seen in the following para-church mission statements.

Local Para-Church Youth Organisation (Scotland)

We are a worldwide fellowship based on the equal value of all persons, respect and freedom for all, tolerance and understanding between people of different opinions and active concern for the needs of the community.

National Para-Church Youth Organisation (Scotland)

We believe that all young people deserve to have a safe place to live and the opportunity to reach their full potential. The vision is of an inclusive Christian Movement, transforming communities so that all young people truly belong, contribute and thrive.

Many Christians will read those mission statements and miss the fact that there is nothing distinctly Christian in them. Although the statements are peppered with words like 'Christian movement' and 'transforming communities' these terms are at best ambiguous and at worst misleading. These mission statements demonstrate a commitment to the values of secular humanism. It is this same value system which promotes a 'tolerance' to any worldview other than a worldview which expresses exclusive truth claims.[70] These are the same values that are being used by secular humanists to justify the present restriction of religious freedom.

These secularised Christian youth work mission statements are not isolated examples; secularised aims and purposes are characteristic of all

---

[70] For more information on this, see Christina Odone's 'No God Zone'

professional Christian youth work. Pughe identifies a number of tensions between *secular* youth work and *Christian* youth work. Not only does Pughe identify tensions, she clearly demonstrates that informal education is incompatible with many of the essential elements of the Christian faith. Pughe informs us that the purposes and methods associated with Christian youth work (and Christianity as a whole) are out with the 'boundaries' of secular youth work and informal education:

> Certain practices have been questioned by reference to both the principles of the faith and of youth work. In a democratic society it is wrong to prevent the expression of beliefs; however, I believe that it would be beneficial for youth work and young people if certain methods and purposes were defined as outside the boundaries of youth work and informal education.[71]

What are these 'purposes' and 'methods' of Christian youth work which Pughe argues are incompatible with the purpose and practice of secular youth work? Pughe draws from the work of many informal educators to demonstrate that it is the Christian faith itself which is incompatible with secular youth work. The issues she identifies have a direct bearing on the authority of scripture, the exclusivity of Christ as the way of salvation, and the Christian belief in one true and living God. It is evident from Pughe's article that these beliefs are incompatible with secular youth work. Yet, not wanting to be accused of being intolerant, she maintains that the Christian faith can still play a role in youth work and informal education,

---

[71] Pughe.

providing Christians are willing to compromise the core convictions of Christianity:

> This does not mean it is inappropriate to present the Christian message. Hubery (1963) asserts that while there is no room in youth work for 'dogmatism or narrow minded indoctrination', there is for 'guides, philosophers and friends' who show 'a way of life that is religious in its truest sense'.[72]

In other words, Christianity is compatible with secular youth work, providing it is presented as one option among many others. Informal education is happy with Christian youth work, providing the Christian faith makes no claims about exclusivity of truth, divine commands or authoritative creeds. However, in order for a Christian to accept this approach to Christian youth work, he must compromise the conviction (at least in practice) that the bible is the Word of God and authoritative for faith and practice. Within the context of Christian youth work, it is okay to present the gospel as *a* way of life, but not *the* way of life. Again, if a Christian accepts this, he must lay aside the clear teaching of the Bible which presents Jesus Christ as the exclusive way of salvation:

> Jesus said to him, "I am the way, and the truth, and the life. No one comes to the Father except through me." (John 14:6)

> And there is salvation in no one else, for there is no other name under heaven given among men by which we must be saved. (Acts 4:12)

---

[72] Pughe.

Many Christian youth workers who believe in the exclusivity of salvation find themselves serving in ministry contexts which are defined by secular values. When this happens, their Christian beliefs are reduced to a personal perspective. Secular youth work philosophy may not lead Christian youth workers to abandon their faith, but it will remove the gospel from a central ministry defining position and place it on the periphery of professional practice. In other words: secularised Christian youth work causes the gospel to be eclipsed by humanistic values; consequently, the unique purpose of Christianity is sacrificed on the altar of secularism.

Having established the incompatibility of secular youth work and Christian youth work, Pughe, drawing on Barnett's work, highlights the unique purpose and role which Christian youth work provides for young people:

> Barnett (1951) argues that Christian youth work is and should remain different from 'secular' youth work, that it is a sacred Christian duty to meet the spiritual needs of young people. Faith sets Christian and non-Christian workers apart providing a unique motivation for Christian workers.[73]

Pughe is identifying that Christian youth work marches to the beat of a different drum. She is also highlighting the important fact that the *motivation* for Christian youth work is unique. Regarding the uniqueness of the role and motivation of Christian youth work, Pughe goes on to say:

> Central to Christian youth work is a sense of vocation, a calling or invitation from God to engage in young

---

[73] Pughe.

people's lives. God is sighted as the sustenance, guidance and inspiration for their work. Christian care for young people is based on the value each individual has as an 'object of God's redeeming love' (Warner 1942:45). The Christian youth worker is seen as a servant of the kingdom of God rather than of a political or social agenda.

Sadly, in the pursuit of funding, accreditation and professionalism, this is a calling that many Christian youth workers have lost sight of. While some Christian youth workers seem to embrace the values of informal education blindly, not realising the implications for Christian mission, others seek to maintain and defend the informal education approach on theological grounds. Many Christian youth workers, who operate within a secular approach, justify their methodology in terms of the Bible's teaching on social justice. Christian youth workers who adopt an informal education approach believe that the teaching of the Bible and the example of Jesus give us grounds for doing so. Danny Brierley is a strong advocate of the informal education approach to Christian youth work. Regarding the values of informal education, he offers the following justification for the syncretisation of sacred and secular values:

> But for me, the significance of these values is that they reflect the example set by Jesus Christ. He was a radical, who practiced social inclusion and challenged oppression. His radical message has been distorted over the years by bland platitudes and intolerant statements. But youth and community work enriches

my faith and practice. The church has much to learn.[74]

Brierley falls into the common trap of approaching the scriptures through the lenses of his own culture; he is reading his own context into the life and ministry of Jesus Christ. As a result, he redefines Jesus in order to make Him fit with the secular values of informal education. Two factors at the heart of the incompatibility between Christianity and informal education are the issues of inclusion and exclusion. Brierley, with one broad sweep, makes Jesus sit incredibly comfortably with the secular understanding of inclusion and exclusion. This should raise some serious questions for biblically-minded Christians.

Brierley fails to distinguish between the secular understanding of inclusiveness and exclusiveness and the biblical understanding of these terms. The secular definitions of exclusion and discrimination are not the same as the Bible's, Jesus', or the church's definitions; this is because the state and the church serve two different purposes.

Brierley ultimately does not seem to recognise that the message of Jesus is both inclusive *and* exclusive. It was Jesus who said: 'Whoever comes to me I will never drive away.' (John 6:3) Yet it was this same Jesus who also declared: 'Unless you believe that I am he you will die in your sins.' (John 8:24) The invitation to the Kingdom is extended to all, but only those who believe in Christ are included; those who do not believe are excluded.

---

[74] Danny Brierley, "Pistols at Dawn" *Children and Young People Now,* www.cypnow.co.uk/news/746446/CHURCH-YOUTH-WORK-pistols-dawn/ (accessed 20th Oct 2004).

Evangelical models of working with young people have often been criticised for focusing on the spiritual needs of young people while neglecting their social, emotional and physical needs. Pughe raises similar concerns about evangelicals, from an informal education perspective:

> This approach has been criticised for promoting middle class morality and narrowing the programme because of its preoccupation with spiritual issues. The content of Evangelical youth work will differ, focusing on Bible study, prayer, and evangelism alongside social activities (Farley 1998). But it has been criticised for over-simplifying the needs of young people, seeing only spiritual and not social ones (Milson 1963).[75]

Pughe's criticisms of evangelical approaches to working with young people, from an informal education perspective, are cutting:

> Evangelical youth workers have been seen as 'indoctrinators' and 'brain washers' whose obsession with conversion reduces their interest in developing self-reliance and maturity, eyes are clouded by ideology they see young people as 'spiritual scalps' . . . Indoctrination is the intentional inculcation of unshakeable beliefs. It seeks to stop growth, and restrict the young person's ability to function autonomously.[76]

It is clear from these quotes that informal education and evangelicalism have different concerns when it comes to working with young people. Informal educators see Christian teachings as a hindrance to young people's development. In

---

[75] Pughe.

[76] Pughe.

response, some evangelical youth workers have raised their own concerns about informal education approaches to youth work:

> Christ does not teach us to support the personal development of young people so that they may realise their full potential. We are instead to call them to repentance and faith, because only in that way can they realise their full potential.[77]

Exploring the plurality of perspectives within Christian youth work is helpful because it identifies that there is a lack of clarity in regards to the purpose of Christian youth work. Some Christian youth workers see Christian youth work in terms of personal development; others believe it is primarily about evangelism and discipleship; and others see it as a combination of informal education and Christian teaching. Pughe highlights that the intense conflict between youth ministry and youth work are closely related to the tensions between Christians who see social action as the priority and those who think evangelism is the priority:

> The debate between the application of Christian evangelism or a broader view of Christian social action to youth work revolves around beliefs, consequently there can be no solution as both sides, in their view, hold equally valid positions, which ultimately rest on statements of faith.[78]

Is Pughe correct when she claims that there is no way to determine the truth regarding the place of evangelism and social action? Is the purpose of Christianity primarily social action or evangelism?

---

[77] Pughe.
[78] Pughe.

Is the divide between Christian youth work and ministry simply a parallel to the social action versus evangelism debate? Should Christian ministry be polarised between social action and evangelism? One thing is clear: the answer cannot be found in youth work theory or youth ministry practice. Pughe argues that there is no way to know the answer because the questions relate to beliefs. She is mistaken; just because the questions relate to beliefs does not mean there is no answer. In order to find the answer, we need to go the source of the beliefs: the scriptures.

We will explore the issue relating to social action versus evangelism in a moment, but before we do, we need to identify the core issues surrounding the conflicting perspectives on the purpose of youth work and ministry.

The deeper issues surrounding Christian youth work and ministry ultimately relate to the question, *who* defines the aims and purposes of Christian youth work and ministry? Who is controlling the steering wheel of Christian youth work and ministry? Many Christian youth work projects and ministries are unaware of the fact that their ministry is being driven by an agenda other than Christ's agenda. In some cases, the work is being driven by a desire for worldly acceptance and popularity. In other instances, as we have demonstrated in this chapter, secular philosophy is in the driver's seat.

We live in days of sophisticated vision statements; the market model dominates even in the arenas of education and church. Marketing techniques dominate the practice of many churches; consequently, the slicker your vision statement the more attractive your ministry will appear.

Vision and direction are essential for any ministry, but if we are involved in *Christian* youth work or ministry, our vision must be rooted in the vision of Christ as it is revealed through the scriptures. What is the overall purpose of Christian youth work and ministry? In order to answer that question, we need to understand the purpose of the Christian faith.

If we claim the work that we do with young people is *Christian,* then the aims, values and methods of our work should reflect the Christian faith. The purpose of Christianity is inextricably linked to the purpose of God the Father in sending his Son into the world, by the power of the Holy Spirit, to rescue, redeem and renew a people for Himself. The purpose of God the Father, His Son Jesus Christ, and the Holy Spirit is expressed in the mission of the church. It is the church of Jesus which is the vehicle through which God's purposes are communicated to a lost and dying world. It is the church which has been tasked with reaching the lost. If Christian youth work and ministry is to be truly Christian, it must be rooted in mission. Mission is not an optional extra for a specialised few; mission is the manifestation of the heart of God and in many places the heart of Christian youth work has been ripped out.

Christian youth workers and youth ministers both consider what they do as mission, yet both models of ministry are in conflict with each other. There are several reasons for this tension, but the most important one is the failure to understand the biblical essence of mission. What is 'mission'? J.I Packer gives a profoundly straightforward definition:

> *Mission* is from the Latin *missio* which means "sending." . . .The universal church . . . is sent into the world to fulfil a definite, defined task . . . The appointed task is twofold. First and fundamentally, is the work of worldwide witness, disciple making and church planting . . . Second . . . to practice deeds of mercy and compassion.[79]

Packer helps clear away much of the smoke that surrounds the social action versus evangelism debate: mission is both word *and* action. To be missional in our approach to working with young people is to understand that we have been 'sent' by Jesus Christ into the world to declare the gospel and demonstrate God's love through deeds of compassion.

Many Christian youth workers understand their vocation in terms of the church's calling to be 'salt and light'. They understand that 'faith without deeds is dead' and that the Christian mandate is not about taking care of the soul while neglecting the body. They also understand that the church of Jesus Christ has a social responsibility. The church is not just called to feed the poor; it is called to challenge unjust social structures which oppress the weak. Consequently, Christian youth work seeks to reach young people on the margins of society in order to help empower them to overcome their social, educational and personal difficulties.

Youth ministry on the other hand is passionate about raising up a generation of 'world-shakers', 'history-makers' and 'risk-takers'. They desire to see young people come to faith in Christ, and become strong disciples who reach their generation with the good news of Jesus Christ.

---

[79] J.I. Packer, *Concise Theology: A Guide to* Historic *Christian Beliefs*, (Wheaton IL: Tyndale, 1993), 223-4.

However it would be overly-simplistic to suggest that Christian youth work does the deeds, and youth ministry engages in evangelism. While evangelism and discipleship are the priority of youth ministry and social action is the emphasis of youth work, there is a very real sense in which both approaches to mission are being carried out in a way that is divorced from the true mission of the Christian church. As Packer demonstrated, Mission is word *and* action; mission consists of declaration *and* deeds. Christian youth work tends to separate the social action from the missional purpose and the gospel message, whereas youth ministry tends to neglect social action and misrepresent the message.

Christian youth work is divorced from true mission because its social action is defined by secular and humanistic definitions of 'justice', 'good', and 'true'. Contrary to popular belief, these are not neutral terms, since they do not mean the same to the humanist as they do to the Christian. Informal educators themselves are aware of the fact that the very professional code of ethics which underpins professional youth work practice is incompatible with the Christian faith:

> Informal education is built on certain values and ideas of 'the good'; a belief in democracy and dialogue; a respect for persons; and a commitment to fairness and equality and critical thinking (Jeffs & Smith 1990 & 1996). If Christian youth work is not inherently contrary to these then a Christian interpretation 'the good' is not problematic. The problem arises where dialogue proves difficult because Christians recognise that theirs is the only truth.[80]

---

[80] Pughe.

What is it that does not sit comfortably with the professional values which underpin secular youth work? It is the Christian commitment to truth. The conflict is ultimately about the authority of God's word versus the philosophy of relativism (rejection of absolute truth claims.) The conflict is about authority: God as ultimate authority or human self-autonomy as ultimate authority.

Understanding the aims and values of informal education should help expel the myth that professional Christian youth work is simply engaged in the practical aspect of mission. You cannot separate the works of mission from the message and motivation of the mission, but this is exactly what informal education's aims and values demand. This is the nature of humanism; it is happy to embrace the, 'Love your neighbour as yourself' but not the, 'There is no other name under heaven by which we can be saved.'

The objectives of secular funders likewise operate within this framework of secular humanistic values, and therefore do not promote the mission of the church but actually conflict with the mission of the church. Many Christian youth workers seem to be under the illusion that they can receive funding and accreditation from secular bodies in order to resource and endorse their works of service without any negative impact on the Christian nature of the work they seek to accomplish. What they don't seem to realise is that accreditation and finances come at a cost: they are not given to support the mission of the church, they are given to advance the secular objectives of the funding and accrediting agency. When this happens, secularism defines the nature of the 'mission' and the Christian youth worker's service is no longer in Jesus' name but has become a servant of secularism.

Youth Ministry

If professional Christian youth work is at one end of the spectrum, it could be argued that youth ministry is at the other. On the surface of things, many youth ministries look extremely successful. They attract large crowds of young people when most churches are experiencing an exodus of youth. They host impressive gigs; worship is vibrant; preaching is motivational and they boast numerous 'decisions for Jesus.' Youth ministry has the tendency to leave us with the impression that while the church is stuck in the past. Youth ministry is innovative and relevant (and has the numbers to prove it).

While professional Christian youth workers are busy losing the battle for distinctly Christian aims, principles and practice, it would be easy to assume that youth ministry has very clear aims and purposes; values and methods that are rooted in the Christian mission. Yet this is a faulty assumption; a closer examination will reveal that youth ministry is not so much enabling the church to reach the world as it is enabling the world to reach the church.

The purpose of the work of Christ was foretold by the Old Testament prophets: 'By his knowledge my righteous servant will justify many.' (Isaiah 53:1: NIV) His purpose was also declared by the angel to Joseph: "You are to give him the name Jesus, because he will save his people from their sins." To save from sin and to make righteous are central to the purposes of God in the sending of his Son into the world. Yet even youth ministry, with all its enthusiastic promotion of the Christian faith, is all too often embarrassingly silent when it comes to this aspect of mission. Instead there is the celebration of Christianity as an alternative way of life, or as a means to discovering purpose or destiny. The reason for this is obvious: youth ministry wants to appeal to young people and issues relating to sin and judgement are unappealing.

The influence of wider culture upon the aims of youth ministry can be seen in the following mission statement:

Youth ministry organisation (Australia)

WHY WE EXIST...
We are a ministry that exists to run programs that reach and appeal to the Youth Generation, pushing the boundaries of Youth Culture, and showing young people that life is excellent with Jesus.

In other words, this Christian youth ministry is largely focused on trying to demonstrate that Christianity is relevant. Consequently, Christian youth ministry presentations are often dynamic, exciting and full of passion and energy. The above mission statement says that 'Life with Jesus is excellent' (and who doesn't want an excellent life?), but what does that actually mean?

There is nothing on earth that compares to following Jesus, yet this is not the image that many people have of the Christian faith. Many view Christianity through the eyes of the secular media and see it as restrictive, irrelevant and outdated. Youth ministry works hard at presenting faith in Jesus in dynamic and exciting terms. To a pleasure-seeking generation that wants to experience life to the full, the Christian life is advertised as offering purpose, pleasure and fulfilment.

There are a number of problems with this approach to reaching out to young people. Firstly, aiming to show young people that 'life with Jesus is excellent,' is not the same thing is explaining the gospel. It is not actually evangelism. In fact, if it is not followed up with a clear explanation of the gospel, it can actually undermine the gospel. How is this possible? If we seek to promote faith in Jesus through trying to show and tell people that 'life with Jesus is excellent' we are actually building our ministry on pragmatism and not truth. In other words, we are saying, 'Hey, Jesus works for me, why don't you give him a try?' True evangelism is about presenting the truth to people's minds in such a way that their conscience and affections are awakened. Youth ministry, like youth work, has a tendency to promote Jesus as *a* way of life, rather than *the* way of life. The focus is on the perceived benefits of the gospel and not the message of the gospel itself.

I have to confess that I too fell into this trap as a Christian youth worker. I was so eager to remove the negative image of church from the minds of young people that I would speak passionately about the benefits of the Christian life. I would emphasise the change that Jesus can bring, the purpose he gives, the hope he imparts. Consequently many young people became interested in this view of Christianity. Many decided that they wanted to become Christians. Christian youth ministry can and does see results when it comes to evangelism. So, what's the problem? Surely if the results are good, it does not matter about the methods? What's the issue? The problem is that it's not the whole truth.

The Christian life comes with a cost. True discipleship means dying to the ways of the world and embracing Jesus as the supreme joy. The Christian life is no guarantee that life will be free from pain. God does not always deliver our expectations, God does not always heal and God does not always answer prayer by sending a miracle. When we only emphasise the perceived positive aspects of the Christian life, we set young people up with an expectation of the Christian life as journey of endless enjoyment rather than a call to faithful endurance. Consequently, when trials come, they don't persevere. In my time as a youth worker I saw a large number of young people make decisions for Christ. These same young people encountered a season of joy, but they quickly fell away when difficulty came. Upon reflection I believe one of the key reasons is that they did not have the gospel fully explained to them. They were only told half the story.

While Christian youth work and youth ministry have taken different approaches, they share similar characteristics. Both approaches have allowed their purpose to be defined by the world rather than The Word. Both approaches have traded the gospel of righteousness for the gospel of relevance. The reasons given for the pursuit of relevance are many; however, continued emphasis on cultural relevance may in fact just be a seductive philosophy which justifies compromise in order to ensure popularity and escape persecution.

If we claim the work that we do with young people is 'Christian', then our work should reflect the Christian faith and mission. If we are serious about grounding our work with young people within the aims of the Christian faith, we will find it difficult to articulate our mission statement in exclusively secular terminology. Before we ask the question: 'How do we make the message relevant?', we must understand what the message is.

Christian youth work and youth ministry reach out to young people with great enthusiasm, but in many places they have forgotten the reason why they are reaching out to young people in the first place. One contemporary song that is sung at Christian youth events is 'I'm not ashamed of the gospel.' by Delirious. Thousands of young people gather in stadiums all over the world and sing this song with passion. On the one hand, this looks encouraging, but when we hear the messages which are preached from many youth ministry platforms, it soon becomes obvious why so many young people are not ashamed of the gospel: they have no idea what the gospel is.

The missional purpose of the Christian faith is powerfully portrayed in Paul's own testimony of his calling:

> But rise and stand upon your feet, for I have appeared to you for this purpose, to appoint you as a servant and witness to the things in which you have seen me and to those in which I will appear to you, delivering you from your people and from the Gentiles—to whom I am sending you to open their eyes, so that they may turn from darkness to light and from the power of Satan to God, that they may receive forgiveness of sins and a place among those who are sanctified by faith in me.' (Acts 26:16-18)

This calling is not just for Paul, it is the calling of the church of Jesus Christ. If we claim to be serving God's purposes in the work that we do with young people, then our work must be deeply rooted in this mandate.

BIBLIOGRAPHY

Bell, Rob *Velvet Elvis: Repainting the Christian Faith*, (New York: Harper Collins, 2005).

Boice. James. Montgomery, Ryken. Phil, *The Doctrines of Grace: Rediscovering the Evangelical Gospel*, (Wheaton Illinois: Crossway, 2002),

DeYoung, Kevin *Don't Call it a Comeback: The Old Faith for a New Day*, (Wheaton IL: Crossway, 2011).

Green, Phil "Bells, Trampolines, Bricks and Youthwork": Crusaders Leaders' Training

Hawthorne, Andy, "Ideas that Change the World", *The Message*, http://www.message.org.uk/ideas-that-change-the-world/ (accessed 9th November 2013).

Jeffs, Tony, Smith K. Mark *Informal Education* (Derbyshire, Education Now Publishing, 1999).

Lucas, Sean. Michael., *Being Presbyterian*, (Philipsburg, New Jersey: P&R Publishing Company, 2006).

Owen, John, *The Holy Spirit: His Gifts and Power,* (Scotland: Christian Heritage Imprint by Christian Focus, 2004).

Packer. J.I., *Concise Theology: A Guide to Historic Christian Beliefs,* (Wheaton IL: Tyndale, 1993).

Packer. J.I, *Knowing God*, (Great Britain: Hodder and Stoughton, 1973).

Piper, John, *Brothers We Are Not Professionals*, (Nashville Tennessee: B&H).

Piper, John., "How to Receive the Gift of the Holy Spirit", 1984.

Pughe. Carole. "Christian Youth work: Evangelism or Social action?"

Sproul R.C., *What does it mean to be born again?*, (Grand Rapids Michigan: Reformation Trust Publishing, 2010).

Spurgeon, Charles, "Witnessing Better than Knowing the Future", A Sermon (No. 2330).

Still, William., *The Letters of William Still*, (Edinburgh: Banner of Truth Trust, 1984).

Stott, John., *The Cross of Christ* (Downers Grove, IL, IVP, 1986).

Stott, John., *The Living Church: Convictions of a Life Long Pastor* (England: IVP, 2007).

Tozer, AW., "Conviction and Pain", *The Alliance*, http://www.cmalliance.org/devotions/tozer?id=20 7 (accessed 13 March 2014).

Trueman, Carl., *The Creedal Imperative*, (Wheaton IL, Crossway, 2012).

Ward, Pete.,*Youth Culture and the Gospel*, (London: Marshall: Pickering, 1992).

Wilson, Kenny, *Young People! Who Needs Them?*, (Cambridge: YTC Press, 2009).

ABOUT THE AUTHOR

John Caldwell is an English and RME teacher and lives in the Scottish Highlands with his wife Laura and two sons, Ethan and Caleb. Prior to entering the teaching profession he worked for Paisley YMCA in a number of projects that reached out to young people throughout Renfrewshire. He also preaches and teaches across a variety of denominations and Christian gatherings throughout Scotland.

If you wish to contact John, you can do so through the following social media:
Blog: www.emergingfree.co.uk
Facebook Author Page:
www.facebook.com/jcaldwellskye
Twitter: twitter.com/jcaldwellskye

CPSIA information can be obtained
at www.ICGtesting.com
Printed in the USA
LVOW04s1454210116

471718LV00024B/1387/P

9 781496 165879